W9-AVH-938

BETRAYAL — OUTRAGE — REVENGE

Cultures clash as settlers venture into the domain of Arizona's fiercely independent Apache bands, resulting in a decades-long cycle of betrayal and retribution.

HONOR AND DUTY VIE WITH GREED, JEALOUSY, AND IGNOBLE INTENT.

Depending on the reader's point of view, self-serving maneuverings either contribute to the settling of the Southwest or further subjugate native peoples. No side — career officers, Apache leaders, Mexican troops, ranchers — has a copyright on treachery, though, in Leo Banks's account of devious dealings that fuel the Apache Wars.

DOUBLE CROSS
DO THE ENDS JUSTIFY THE MEANS?

Read these stories of Cochise and Lieutenant Bascom, Chief Eskiminzin, General George Crook, Geronimo, the Apache scouts, and General Nelson Miles. And then decide.

Other books in the
WILD WEST COLLECTION
showcase fast-paced, real-life stories of when the Old West was still young and rowdy, where anything could happen — and too often did.

DAYS OF DESTINY
MANHUNTS & MASSACRES
THEY LEFT THEIR MARK
THE LAW OF THE GUN
TOMBSTONE CHRONICLES
STALWART WOMEN
INTO THE UNKNOWN
RATTLESNAKE BLUES
BUCKSKINS, BEDBUGS & BACON

Turn to the back of this book to learn more about them.

Design: MARY WINKELMAN VELGOS
Production: BETH ANDERSON
Photographic enhancement: BETH ANDERSON
Front cover art: GARY BENNETT
Tooled leather design on covers: KEVIN KIBSEY AND RONDA JOHNSON
Production Coordinator: KIM ENSENBERGER
Copy editor: EVELYN HOWELL
Book editors: BOB ALBANO AND PK PERKIN McMAHON

FRONT COVER ART:
The illustration depicts Cochise cutting his way to freedom from a tent to
which he had been lured by an Army lieutenant intent on arresting the
Chiricahua Apache Chief for the kidnapping of a young boy in southeastern
Arizona. See Chapter Two.

Published by the Book Division of *Arizona Highways*® magazine, a monthly
publication of the Arizona Department of Transportation, 2039 West Lewis
Avenue, Phoenix, Arizona 85009. Telephone: (602) 712-2200
Web site: www.arizonahighways.com

Publisher — Win Holden
Managing Editor — Bob Albano
Associate Editors — Evelyn Howell and PK Perkin McMahon
Art Director — Mary Winkelman Velgos
Production Director — Cindy Mackey

Copyright© 2001 by Arizona Department of Transportation, State of Arizona.
All rights reserved under International and Pan-American copyright
conventions. Except for quotations used in articles, reviews, and book listings,
no part of this book may be reproduced in any form by any electronic or
mechanical means, including information storage and retrieval systems,
without written permission from the publisher.

Printed in the United States
Library of Congress Catalog Number 2001130363
ISBN 1-893860-23-X

DOUBLE CROSS

Treachery in the Apache Wars

by LEO W. BANKS

ARIZONA HIGHWAYS
B O O K S

DEDICATION

*To my son Patrick, who could tell Geronimo
a thing or two.*

**WELL-ARMED APACHE SCOUTS AT SAN CARLOS
DURING THE 1880S.**

L eo W. Banks's fascination with the Apache Wars began with the books and magazines he read as a child, and of course, with Hollywood Westerns. But these sources were rarely accurate. In 25 years of writing about, and traveling extensively through Arizona, the truth has come into much sharper focus.

This book represents the culmination of that long process of finding out what really happened.

Leo graduated from Boston College with a degree in history in 1975, and earned a master's degree in journalism from the University of Arizona in 1977.

He began his career as a feature writer for the *Arizona Daily Star* in Tucson, and has worked as a correspondent for the *Boston Globe* and the *Los Angeles Times*, covering stories in small towns around Arizona. For the past decade, he has written many articles for *Arizona Highways* magazine, and several books for the magazine's book division.

These include *Stalwart Women* and *Rattlesnake Blues*, both of which told of life in Arizona Territory. He co-wrote *Grand Canyon Stories*, was one of five authors of *Travel Arizona II*, a guidebook, and was a major contributor to both *Days of Destiny* and *Manhunts & Massacres*, also part of the Wild West Collection.

His freelance articles have appeared in *Sports Illustrated*, *The Wall Street Journal*, *National Geographic Traveler* and numerous other publications.

He lives in Tucson with his wife, Teresa, and six-year-old son, Patrick.

C O N T E N T S

DURING SURRENDER NEGOTIATIONS, APACHE LEADER
GERONIMO, RIGHT, WITH HIS SON AND TWO WARRIORS,
POSED FOR PHOTOGRAPHER C.S. FLY.

Treachery and Betrayal

Treachery was a driving force in the Apache Wars. By this I mean that many of the significant events in the subjugation of the Indians — or the settling of the Southwest, depending on your point of view — were decided according to the old-fashioned double cross. Most of the 13 chapters in this book deal with a specific episode of betrayal.

In this category I included the story of a scalp hunter, who, during a trading session in 1837, turned a cannon on an Apache chief and his band. Also included is the story two decades later of the bumbling young lieutenant who wrongfully accused Cochise of kidnapping a rancher's son, thus touching off 10 years of killing in retribution.

Other chapters focus on such incidents as Geronimo breaking his promise to surrender in Canyon de los Embudos in 1885; the murder of the gallant Capt. Emmet Crawford by Mexican irregulars, supposed allies in the fight against the Apaches; and the defection of an Indian nicknamed Peaches, who handed American troops a stunning success by guiding them into the Mexican stronghold of renegade Apaches.

And when seven soldiers died in an uprising at Cibecue Creek in eastern Arizona in 1881 — the largest number of troopers killed in any encounter between Indians and soldiers in Arizona Territory history — the villains in that extraordinary episode were mutinous Army scouts.

Other chapters deal less with specific episodes than with trends. The decision, for example, by hundreds of Indians to turn on their own people and fight with the soldiers was decisive in the war's outcome.

One chapter tells of Gen. George Crook's Winter Campaign of 1872-73, the first to make significant use of Indian scouts, and the impact they had on his success.

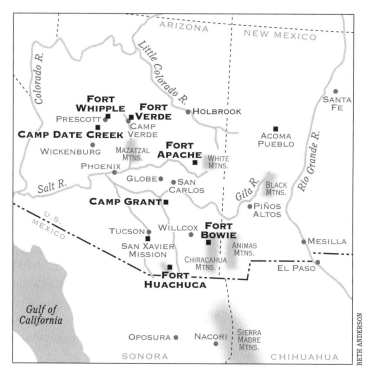

THE GEOGRAPHICAL SCOPE OF THE APACHE WARS.

Another describes the bitter feud between Crook and his successor, Gen. Nelson Miles, in the war's aftermath. Miles's effort to grab credit for the final Apache surrender, and hide his use of Crook's methods in achieving it, was certainly a betrayal of Crook, and in a broader sense, of what soldiers like to call military decorum.

The final chapter tells the story of Massai, a former Army scout who escaped from the train taking Apaches to their imprisonment in Florida at war's end. He made his way back to the Southwest and lived 20 more years as an outlaw in the mountains.

The more I thought about Massai as a subject for a book on betrayals, the more perfect he seemed. He was, after all, the ultimate betrayer and outcast, unable to stay with his own people, or with the scouts, and surely not on Miles's prison train.

In deciding which episodes to recount, I studied — and ultimately quoted from — a number of historians and authors who focused on the Apache Wars, among them: Odie Faulk, Dan Thrapp, Frank Lockwood, Peter DeMontravel, and Louis Kraft.

I was helped as well by generous researchers and writers, such as Britt Wilson, of Banning, Calif., who supplied some long-buried reports and good counsel about the early 1870s; Tucsonan Chuck Collins, who offered guidance on the Cibecue chapter; and others.

Edwin Sweeney, the noted biographer of both Cochise and Mangas Coloradas, sent along crucial bits of information and paperwork I was unable to locate on my own, and Tucson writer Jeanie Marion shared her expertise on the Aravaipa Apache Chief Eskiminzin. I gratefully acknowledge their help.

— Leo W. Banks

CHAPTER ONE

Friendship's Bounty

*Chief Compa had intercepted dispatches giving him
advance knowledge of Johnson's plans; but he
could not believe that his friend Johnson could
possibly entertain any project against his life.*

———◆———

THE BOOM OF A SCOUNDREL'S CANNON SIGNALED THE FIRST
salvo in what would become nearly 50 years of warfare
pitting Mexicans and Americans against Apaches. The
gun was fired on April 22, 1837, in what is now Hidalgo County,
New Mexico, by a scalp hunter and trader named John Johnson.

If the story is true in its standard telling, as most historians believe, Johnson's murdering some 20 Chiricahua Apaches
that day, including Chief Juan Jose Compa, supposedly his friend,
was among the most calculating the frontier had seen.

After Johnson had set his trap and fired the first volley,
Compa appealed to his friend's sense of loyalty and begged him
to stop the bloodshed.

Johnson responded by shooting the chief dead at close
range. How else, Johnson no doubt reasoned, could he collect
the bounty offered by Mexican government officials on Apache
scalps? However, as with every episode in the Apache conflict,
this seemingly simple story of betrayal for money requires some
understanding of the times in which it occurred.

The Mexican states of Chihuahua and Sonora had been
under siege by Apache raiders, to varying degrees, for more than
two decades. The trouble had escalated throughout the 1820s,
and after 1831 it expanded into a general, though sporadic, war.

Its effects on the northern regions of Sonora and
Chihuahua were profound. One historian, Ralph Smith, wrote

that Mexican literature "bulges with heartbreaking stories of woodcutters slain in the forests, sheepherders shot down in the pastures, workmen cut up in fields, travelers left along the road bristling with arrows, and settlers slumped in doorways of their mud, straw, and stick huts.

"Still more pathetic," said Smith in a 1962 issue of the *New Mexico Historical Review*, "were the tales of women and children dragged off into their captivity."

A presidio commander in Sonora estimated that Apaches killed 5,000 Mexicans between 1820 and 1835 and forced the abandonment of a hundred mining camps, ranches, and other settlements. "Nothing was left but the demoralized garrisons of worthless soldiers," reported Ignacio Zuniga.

The situation in Chihuahua was little better, according to Frank Lockwood. In his book, *The Apache Indians*, he wrote: "The savages became so daring that they would appear in bands of only three or four on the very outskirts of the city of Chihuahua in open day, kill the herders and field laborers, and drive off herds of horses and mules unmolested."

The Mexican central government, in its supreme disorganization and lack of concern for troubles on the frontier, did little to protect its people. When Mexican forces did engage the Apaches in battle, they won occasional victories but more often found the Indians both mobile and stealthy — a tough foe.

The Mexicans, said Lockwood, also found them well-armed, due to their trading for weapons with American trappers and the theft of arms from their victims.

Several attempts at truces were made during the 1830s, but each, inevitably, collapsed. One reason was the great distrust between the two sides. Another was that each Chiricahua band operated more or less independently, meaning an agreement entered into by one band wouldn't be honored by others.

Mexican leaders also erred in not providing food and provisions to the Apaches, who traditionally had acquired such necessities through raiding.

One notable treaty, signed in August 1832 between Jose

Joaquin Calvo, the military *commandante* of Chihuahua, and 29 chieftains, divided Apache country into three zones, each commanded by a chief called a general. One of the zones was based at the presidio of Janos under the command of Juan Jose Compa.

But the agreement disintegrated within months, due in part to Calvo's unwillingness to give provisions to the Apaches. He also refused to include Sonora in the pact, so the Apaches could simply cross into that state to kill and raid to acquire what they needed.

By 1835, the situation had grown so desperate that Sonoran Governor Jose Escalante y Arvizu announced his *proyecto de guerra* — or plan of war. In addition to other provisions, it offered fortune seekers 100 pesos for the scalp of every Apache warrior age 14 or older. This policy was directly responsible for the Johnson massacre, according to the account of the episode most historians have relied upon. Its author, Benjamin D. Wilson, worked as a trapper in New Mexico in the mid-1830s, and maintained friendly relations with Compa.

The chief was well known at that time, although he was not considered a particularly influential Chiricahua leader. Born in about 1785, as a boy he attended a Spanish presidio school where, in Wilson's words, he became "quite an educated man," with the ability "to read, write, and keep accounts."

As did most Chiricahuas, Compa hated Mexicans. Also like most Chiricahuas, he initially maintained good relations with Americans. In a narrative of his adventures on the frontier that Wilson dictated in 1877, he observed that Compa "never lost an opportunity to show them his friendship."

"Whenever by any mistake any animals belonging to American parties were stolen by Apaches," Wilson wrote, "Juan Jose would have them returned to the owners."

The chief's eagerness to maintain good relations with Americans — probably because Apaches were able to trade with them for arms — extended to Wilson, who had no permission to trap in Mexican territory. He was therefore considered a smuggler or interloper who would have fared badly if discovered. But he never was, thanks to Compa.

"Juan Jose was frequently in our camp and had mails brought to him to read, which had been captured by his men," Wilson reported in his narrative, published in 1934 by the Historical Society of Southern California. "We thus became informed of the military movements contemplated by the Mexican government. . . . Juan Jose's friendship was in every way valuable to us."

By 1837, John Johnson had been trading between Sonora and New Mexico for several years and in that time had been well-treated by the Apaches.

A hatter by trade, he came west in 1827 and soon began trading around Sonora. Johnson married a Mexican woman, and they had four sons and operated a ranch and trading post in Oposura, Sonora — which, after 1828, became Moctezuma. He is sometimes identified as Henry Johnson, and Wilson called him James Johnson.

Working in concert with another American named Gleason or Glisson, Johnson set out from Oposura on April 3, 1837, to make money from Apache heads, according to Wilson.

His party consisted of five Mexicans and 17 Americans. Twelve of the latter had ridden into Mexico, led by a Missourian named Eames, to purchase mules. They found that the Apaches had stripped the country of them and were returning home through Sonora when they met Johnson.

He promised to show them a good route back, which would bring them past Compa's camp. According to Wilson, the Eames party was thus brought unknowingly into Johnson's scheme.

Historian Rex Strickland, one of the few to examine the episode and sympathize with Johnson, agreed with Wilson that the Missouri men had no knowledge of a plot to kill the chief because, he said, there most likely wasn't one.

In his alternative version, published in *Arizona and the*

West in 1976, Strickland argued that Johnson wasn't after Compa's scalp. Rather, he was pursuing, with official sanction from the Sonoran government, the perpetrators of a deadly Apache raid late in March at Noria, 30 miles north of Oposura.

Johnson's payment, according to the terms of his agreement with Sonora, wasn't for Compa's scalp. The scalp-bounty law of 1835 was no longer in effect in 1837. Rather, Johnson was after half of the booty he took from Compa, which, according to the agreement, he would be allowed to keep.

The Noria trouble occurred about the same time the Missouri party arrived in Sonora. Finding no mules, these men agreed to accompany Johnson on a counter-raid, hoping to secure the animals from the Apaches, according to Strickland.

The Missourians were led by Bill Knight and Charles Ames, who probably was the same man that Wilson identified as Eames. Strickland asserted that the man Wilson named as Gleason or Glisson, was actually Benjamin Leaton, a notorious frontiersman.

Johnson's men arrived at Compa's camp in the Animas Mountains, located in present-day southwestern New Mexico, on April 20.

As it happened, Compa had intercepted dispatches giving him advance knowledge of Johnson's plans. But according to Wilson, Compa "could not believe that Johnson, whose friend he had ever been, could possibly entertain any project against his life."

Compa related what he had learned to his friend Johnson. "Don Santiago," Compa said to Johnson, "you have never deceived me, and if you give me your word of honor that the report is false, come to my camp with your men and pass the night with us."

Johnson gave his assurance and told the chief he had a sack of *pinole* (dried, roasted corn) to give to the women and children.

The two groups traded freely for two days. On the night

before the third day, as Johnson planned his treachery, the five Mexicans in his group departed from the camp, wanting no part of the impending attack.

At 10 o'clock on the morning of the third day, as the Chiricahuas began picking through the bags of *pinole*, Johnson unveiled a small swivel cannon loaded with balls, slugs, and scrap-iron. His plan was for Gleason to lure Compa from the main group on the pretext of wanting to buy the chief's saddle mule. Then, when the cannon was fired into the group, Gleason was to kill Compa with his pistol.

"This hellish plot was carried out to the letter, the blunderbuss was fired into the crowd, killing and maiming many," reported Wilson, who later became the first American mayor of Los Angeles and the namesake of California's Mount Wilson.

"Gleason shot at Juan Jose but did not kill him, the latter [Compa] cried out to his friend, Don Santiago, to come to his aid, and clenched Gleason, and had him down, with a knife drawn, [and speaking in Spanish told Johnson]: 'For God's sake, save my life! I could kill your friend, but I don't want to do it!'

"Johnson's only reply was to shoot Juan Jose whilst he was over Gleason, with his knife drawn. Juan Jose fell dead on Gleason."

Johnson's party then took aim on the wounded and panicked Apaches, killing as many as they could, including women and children.

Wilson concluded his comments on Juan Jose Compa this way: "Thus perished that fine specimen of a man. I knew the man well, and could vouch for the fact that he was a perfect gentleman, as well as a kind-hearted one."

Strickland's version, again, represents an alternative. He said that Johnson was unaware until his arrival in the camp that it was Compa's, and that it was later that Johnson found out — although Strickland doesn't specify how — that Compa's band was responsible for the raid at Noria.

Moreover, Johnson was moved to attack, said Strickland,

after hearing of Compa's own plot against the Americans, a story told him by a Mexican girl named Autora.

She had been stolen by the Apaches and was purchased back by Johnson on the afternoon of the second day, after which she informed Johnson that Compa planned to ambush the trader and his men.

This information, a direct contradiction to Wilson's claim that Compa desired friendship with Americans, came from a letter Johnson wrote to Chihuahuan leader Jose Joaquin Calvo a few days after the episode. In it, he noted — somewhat conveniently, critics say — that Autora saw "acts of mistrust and treachery" from Compa's band.

In desperation, outnumbered five to one, Johnson decided to attack, Strickland said. The ensuing fight lasted two hours.

Strickland's criticism of Wilson's account as inaccurate in parts, and overly melodramatic, is probably warranted. Wilson claimed, for instance, that Oposura was so besieged by Apaches after the massacre that Johnson couldn't remain there and had to sell his property and flee to California.

Actually, the opposite was true. He remained in Oposura, living as a prominent businessman and hero to Mexicans, who saw his act as just retaliation against a brutal band. He even was the subject of a laudatory folk ballad.

But most historians find Strickland's claims about Johnson's motives less convincing. They note that even though Sonora's scalp-bounty law was no longer officially in effect in 1837, Johnson nevertheless promised to deliver scalps to the *commandante-general* of Sonora.

And Johnson did indeed take the scalps of Compa; his brother, Chief Juan Diego; and another chief named Marcelo. As it turned out, Johnson and his men each were paid 100 pesos by the state of Chihuahua, under Calvo, which had begun offering scalp bounties as well. Those who favor the Wilson version believe that Johnson calculated, certainly correctly, that he knew he would be paid for the scalps one way or the other.

Another factor lending credence to the Wilson version was the Chiricahuas' reaction of pure outrage, which probably wouldn't have occurred following a defeat in ordinary battle.

Through the use of smoke and runners, word of the massacre spread quickly to other Apache bands, which massed in an effort to kill Johnson. They failed, but the party was forced to fight their way to Janos, and eventually Oposura.

Next, Apaches massacred a party of 22 trappers led by Charles Kemp, and the Indians attacked a wagon train at a place called Point of Rocks en route from Santa Fe to El Paso, killing 12 more.

Wilson himself barely escaped retribution. At the time of the Compa massacre, he and several other men were camped 30 miles away on the Gila River. Two weeks later they were making their way back to Santa Fe, unaware of the killings, when Apaches took them prisoner.

Wilson and his two partners — identified only as Maxwell and Tucker — were astonished at the "changed conduct of the Apaches" and soon learned that something terrible had happened, although they had no specifics. They were stripped of their clothing and confined in the Apache camp.

The young warriors wanted to kill the three and kept up a war dance that night. Chief Mangas Coloradas, eager to continue friendly relations with Americans, opposed his warriors' plans, but even as chief, his power to stop them was limited.

Late that night, as the warriors gathered wood to burn the three men alive, Mangas, "greatly excited," arranged for Wilson's escape. Wearing only a small buffalo robe, Wilson eventually made his way, on foot, all the way to Santa Fe.

While there, Wilson heard the story of Compa's death from the Missourian he called Eames. Tucker and Maxwell also managed to escape, perhaps in the excitement caused by the warriors' hunt for Wilson.

By then, all of northern Mexico was defending itself against the rampaging Chiricahuas. The Mexicans, of course, never understood that the Indians believed they were operating out of self-defense as well. After all, Sonora's scalp-hunting policy was essentially one of extermination, and it was closely followed by Chihuahua's, which brought an army of disreputable men into the country for the sole purpose of killing Apaches.

The grisly trade only made the Chiricahuas more fierce in defending their land and people. Johnson's treachery, especially his willingness to kill women and children, did the same.

It scratched a time line in the dirt after which, in the words of noted historian Arthur Woodward, "the land which was to become the territories of Arizona and New Mexico was seldom at peace."

CHAPTER TWO

The Bascom Affair

*Cochise fled through a phalanx of Army riflemen
who fired after him as he raced over a hilltop, his
coffee cup still in hand. Later, he reappeared and
shouted to Bascom, asking to see his brother,
Coyuntura. Bascom answered with gunfire.*

———◆———

C OCHISE'S WAR ERUPTED WITH EXQUISITE FURY IN 1861,
24 years after the Johnson massacre. The episode that
sparked it, known as the Bascom Affair, has been analyzed,
reconstructed, and tipped upside down more than any other in
relations between whites and Apaches. Yet the events remain
cloudy.

Eyewitnesses and those who came on the scene within
days differ in their accounts, although the reader can sense in
their words an awareness that what they saw and described
was momentous.

This was a drama that could not be invented. Its two central players shared little in common except for an outsized
pride — a belief in their own importance — and those feelings
could only drive events to no good end.

Kentucky-born George N. Bascom graduated from the
United States Military Academy at West Point in 1858, finishing an unspectacular 26th in a class of 27. He had been an
Army lieutenant in Arizona for five months when he was ordered to Apache Pass to retrieve a kidnapped boy. Not yet 25
years old, Bascom was supremely stubborn and, we can presume, derived much of what he believed about Apaches from his
imagination.

The Chiricahua leader Cochise was a revered figure among

LT. GEORGE NICHOLAS BASCOM, LIKE MANY OFFICERS
IN THE APACHE WARS, GRADUATED FROM WEST POINT.

his people, their absolute leader. Approximately 50 years old at
the time, intelligent, tall, with well-chiseled features, he had
three brass rings in each ear, and projected a dignity that could
cow the toughest man.

But when crossed, as he was by Bascom, he became what
Indian-haters believed he was — savage.

These two adversaries came together on February 4, 1861.
The month before, Apaches had raided a ranch in the
Sonoita Valley of what is now southeastern Arizona, driving
off some cattle and stealing the 12-year-old step-son of ranch
owner John Ward.

Based on tracks, both Ward and Arizona's military leaders assumed the raiders were bound for Apache Pass, a crucial divide on the route to California, between the Dos Cabezas
and Chiricahua mountains. The pass was home to Cochise and
his band, so they were presumed guilty.

Bascom and 54 men of the 7th Infantry rode out of Fort
Buchanan, south of Tucson near Patagonia, with orders to do
what was propr to recover the stock and the boy, Felix Ward,

DOUBLE CROSS

AN ARTIST'S RENDERING OF CHIRICAHUA CHIEFTAIN COCHISE.

and in the bargain "to pursue and chastise such marauding parties."

The soldiers arrived at the Overland stage station in Apache Pass on Sunday, February 3. After sending word to Cochise requesting a meeting, Bascom headed into Siphon Canyon, three-quarters of a mile away, to make camp.

Late the following day, Cochise arrived with his wife; his younger brother, Coyuntura; two of his children; and two or three warriors, possibly his nephews. Historians believe his decision to bring family members indicates that he anticipated no trouble, having had nothing to do with the Ward raid.

Exactly what transpired inside Bascom's tent that day remains somewhat mysterious. The likeliest version, based on several accounts, is that Bascom served dinner to Cochise, his brother, and one of his nephews. Then after friendly talk, the lieutenant turned accuser, naming Cochise as the perpetrator of the raid.

The chief denied it. He said the boy had been taken by members of the Coyoteros band, who held him captive in the Black Mountains. Cochise then offered to try to bring Felix Ward in, if Bascom were willing to remain at the stage station for 10 days.

But that wouldn't do for the lieutenant, who firmly believed Cochise was responsible and had plotted all along to take the chief prisoner. As soon as Cochise had entered the tent, Bascom's soldiers surrounded it to prevent escape.

After Cochise's offer, the lieutenant announced that the chief and his people would be held hostage until the boy was returned. Enraged, Cochise drew his knife, slashed open the back of the tent and fled, with his brother and one warrior following.

In the account of an eyewitness, a soldier known only as Oberly, Bascom yelled, "Shoot them down!"

What happened to the first two escapees is unclear. Oberly said Coyuntura was stopped by a bullet through the leg. Another memoirist reported that one of them was knocked to the ground with the butt of a carbine and the second bayoneted, but survived. This much is certain: neither one escaped.

The third, Cochise, fled through a phalanx of Army riflemen. An estimated 50 shots were fired as he raced over a hilltop, his coffee cup still in hand. Shortly thereafter, he reappeared and shouted down to Bascom, asking to see his brother, Coyuntura. Bascom answered with gunfire.

At that, the chief raised his hand, swore revenge, and shouted, "Indian blood is as good as white man's blood!" Then he left.

The conflicting versions of this incident, as with several that followed, usually break down according to whether the teller supports the officer's actions or finds them reprehensible. Even today, Bascom personifies whatever viewpoint a chronicler wishes to expound.

Oberly's recollections provide a case in point. Writing 25 years after the fact, he depicted Cochise as entirely friendly with Americans prior to this encounter, but that portrayal wasn't quite true. Furthermore, he was highly critical of Bascom, saying that the lieutenant was "totally unfit to deal with the Apaches." He alone among memoirists implied that Bascom was a drunk, "well-supplied with commissary whiskey, which he used liberally."

Oberly concluded — correctly on this point — that Cochise and his party had done absolutely nothing wrong, and "came into camp on a friendly invitation from Bascom and without fear of molestation."

On the other hand, writing in 1887, B.J.D. Irwin, an assistant military surgeon who arrived at Apache Pass six days after the tent episode, described Bascom and other Americans as victims of the cowardly and wicked Chiricahua chief. He said the lieutenant announced that he was keeping Cochise and his people only as a last resort, "after every effort at peaceful persuasion had proved futile."

Adding to the murkiness surrounding the incident, Edwin Sweeney, Cochise's biographer, claimed that Bascom lied in his official report to his superiors by saying he had consented to Cochise's proposition.

If he had, an escape obviously wouldn't have been necessary. Sweeney said that all six of the written recollections of the incident by Americans concur that Cochise was not released, but escaped.

Looking back, Bascom had good reason to lie. He was embarrassed at losing the man he believed responsible for the Ward raid, thus touching off several days of spectacular violence.

Bascom moved his command back to the Overland stage station, perhaps thinking that its rock walls would help protect his soliders in the fight he believed was coming. On the morning after he had fled from the tent, Cochise appeared on the hill south of the station, accompanied by a Coyotero chief named

Francisco and about 500 warriors. They presented a white flag of truce and asked to talk with Lieutenant Bascom.

Four men from each party moved cautiously together, converging about 150 yards from the station. The meeting went nowhere. Cochise pleaded for the release of his family, and Bascom again insisted that Cochise return the Ward boy first.

Then the unexpected happened. Three civilian Overland employees — James Wallace, Charles Culver, and a third man identified only as Walsh or Welch — believing their existing friendship with Cochise might break the stalemate, moved forward among the Indians, ignoring Bascom's order to stay back.

When warriors concealed in a ravine rushed forward to capture the three, shooting broke out. Culver knocked down two of his Indian captors and broke for the stage station, along with Welch. Culver reached the front door before taking a bullet in the back and collapsing, severely injured. At the station's stone corral, Welch popped his head above the rocks, whereupon a soldier on the other side, mistaking him for an Apache, shot him through the head, killing him instantly. Wallace remained a captive.

One of the unarmed soldiers who accompanied Bascom, also unarmed, to the parlay was wounded in the turmoil, and according to Irwin, one bullet passed through Bascom's clothing and another through his hat.

Several Apaches probably were wounded as well, and a few were killed. That night, in the words of Sgt. Daniel Robinson, who told his version in the August 1896 issue of *Sports Afield*, the "weird war cries of the squaws were distinctly heard wailing over their dead."

At noon the following day, Cochise again tried to make an exchange. This time he appeared on a hill above the station dragging a hungry and freezing Wallace behind him, the captive's hands tied behind his back and a rope looped around his neck. The chief asked for his family back in exchange for Wallace and 16 government mules.

But Bascom's answer hadn't changed — he wanted the Ward boy returned.

Here dissension might have split Bascom's command, according to a controversial story told by Reuben Bernard, a sergeant in the 1st Dragoons. He claimed he was at Bascom's side that day and mounted a bitter protest against the lieutenant's decision to reject Cochise's deal.

In his telling, published in a 1936 book titled *One Hundred and Three Fights and Skirmishes, the Story of General Reuben F. Bernard*, Bernard said he protested in an effort to rescue Wallace.

"Damn it, Lieutenant, here's a man whose life is at stake."

After more arguing, Bascom supposedly responded, "Sergeant, you are insubordinate. Consider yourself under arrest."

Bernard maintained that the insubordination charges against him were not pushed vigorously, and he was acquitted. But no record of any court-martial has been found, and significantly, records indicate that the 1st Dragoons did not arrive at Apache Pass until eight days after the encounter described by Bernard.

Bernard also stated that Cochise held two other white men as well, and that Bascom was unwilling to make the trade, unless it was for all three. But his chronology is wrong.

Cochise didn't take additional prisoners until that night, when his men waylaid a 12-man wagon train hauling flour through the pass to New Mexico. The Chiricahuas considered nine of them worthy of execution on their nationality alone — they were Mexicans. The Indians tied the men by their wrists to the wagon wheels, tortured them, and then set fire to the wagons.

Cochise kept the three Americans — not two as Bernard said — as trade bait. They were Sam Whitfield, William Sanders, said to be a half-breed Cherokee, and Frank Brunner, a German teamster.

Also that same night, February 6, Cochise returned to the hill overlooking the stage station and left a note for Bascom. It was written by Wallace in charcoal, according to William

Sanders Oury, an Overland employee, and attached to a stake driven into the ground.

"Treat my people well and I will do the same by yours, of whom I have three." In truth, by then, it was four — Wallace, Whitfield, Sanders, and Brunner.

Several chroniclers have made the same mistake as Bernard in handing Cochise more prisoners than he actually had at noon on February 6. But as wrong as Bernard was on that point, his claim of having been present cannot be ruled out.

He might have been sent there as part of a detachment prior to the arrival after the tent incident of the main body of dragoons, and, as historian Dan Thrapp observed, an insubordination charge against Bernard might have been handled by a summary court-martial, a type that would not have been a matter for written record.

Why Bascom didn't get Wallace's note remains a mystery. But for Cochise, the silence from the lieutenant was an answer to his offer, an unspoken death sentence for the four hostages.

Early the morning of February 7, the Apaches attempted to waylay another eastbound stage in the pass, apparently to secure more hostages. Although the Overland driver had his leg broken by a rifle bullet, the effort failed and the coach reached the station about 2 A.M.

During this time, according to Oberly, Bascom became thoroughly unnerved, cowering behind the stone walls, afraid even to permit his parched soldiers to go for water at the spring nearby.

Finally, after Sergeant Robinson safely filled six canteens, Oberly said, "Bascom's craven fears were stilled and he ordered the mules taken to the water but they were attacked" as they returned by a party of naked Indians, painted and singing a war song.

"Like a flash the entire place was filled with Indians," said Oberly of the February 8 fight. "They seemed to spring from the earth."

"They were coming so openly and boldly that they no

doubt expected to sweep all before them without much trouble," according to Robinson.

The sergeant was wounded in the shooting, a station employee killed, and the raiders made off with 56 mules. But the attack at the spring served only as a diversion.

The main raid, meant to overrun the station and free Cochise's relatives, was under way, probably led by Cochise himself. A young Geronimo, then 38, and Chief Mangas Coloradas and his band also were present. But this force was driven off, too, by heavy fire from behind the stone walls.

With his failure to capture the station, Cochise gave up hope of retrieving his relatives and headed into Mexico. Bascom and his men, unaware of this, stayed put for six days, keenly awaiting the next Chiricahua raid.

In the meantime, in response to a dispatch sent by Bascom on February 7, two relief columns were en route to Apache Pass. One was a volunteer group of 14 men, led by assistant surgeon B.J.D. Irwin out of Fort Buchanan.

En route, as his party crossed a dry lake south of the present town of Willcox, they encountered a Coyotero chief and two warriors herding 30 stolen ponies and 40 head of cattle. Irwin wrote that "after a long and exciting chase and a running fight, extending over several miles," he captured the Indians and the stock.

He drove the animals ahead of his command to Apache Pass, where their arrival on February 10 was "hailed with shouts of joy, as it was feared that the expected relief party had been intercepted and wiped out."

Two companies of dragoons, led by Lieutenant Moore, arrived four days later from Fort Breckenridge (later named Camp Grant). With these reinforcements, scouting parties rode into the mountains, but they encountered no Apaches.

On February 18, however, the scouting soldiers spotted buzzards hovering in the sky, and riding to the scene, a small valley on the west side of the Chiricahuas, they found the horribly mutilated bodies of Cochise's four prisoners — Wallace,

Whitfield, Sanders and Brunner. Writing in 1877, primarily in defense of Bascom, Oury, who was present, said that only "by the gold filling in some of his teeth" was he able to identify Wallace. "All the bodies were literally riddled with lance holes," he said.

The remains were taken to a mound studded with oak trees and buried. On the trip back to the station, Oury said the shaken command decided to hang all the Indians held by Bascom "to the trees that shaded our new-made grave."

After unsaddling his horse, Moore relayed his decision to Bascom, who objected, believing he would face the censure of his superiors. But Oury said that Moore, as ranking officer, told Bascom he would assume all responsibility.

In his typescript, however, Irwin said the decision to hang the Indians was made at his initiative. "It was I who suggested," he wrote with evident pride, "their summary execution, man for man."

When Bascom objected, Irwin claimed the right to execute the three prisoners he had taken, regardless of what Bascom did. At that, the lieutenant relented.

The three Coyoteros most likely had nothing to do with the Cochise-Bascom standoff. Irwin would later receive the Medal of Honor for their capture.

The next day, Moore, Irwin, and Bascom departed Apache Pass. When they reached the fresh graves of the four Americans, the soldiers stopped. Bascom led the six Indians to the oak trees and told them what was about to happen.

The condemned men, according to Oberly, wanted to be shot instead of hanged, and they asked for whiskey. Both requests were denied.

The *Mesilla Times*, a New Mexico newspaper, reported that one of the Indians, probably Coyuntura, went to the gallows "dancing and singing, saying that he was satisfied that he had killed two Mexicans in that month."

"Another," the paper said, [was] "begging piteously for his life" before, as Robinson said, he and his fellows were "hoisted so high by the infantry that even the wolves could not touch them."

Cochise's wife and two sons — including Naiche, who would become a chief himself and bedevil the Army in the war's last days — were subsequently turned loose. But even this seemingly simple fact was layered in legend, this one created by Cochise himself.

In October 1870, William F. Arny, an Indian agent in New Mexico, summoned the southern Apache bands for a peace council, drawing some 790 members and their chiefs. Among them was Cochise, with whom Arny talked for several hours.

In his version of the Apache Pass trouble, described by Arny in the *Santa Fe Weekly New Mexican* for November 1, 1870, the chief said that "two officers played a game of cards to determine whether the children should be hung, [and] that the one who opposed hanging won the game."

Cochise also told Arny that the events of those two weeks so outraged him that he went on the warpath and had been fighting ever since. His explanation has been accepted by historians as the effective start of the Apache Wars with Americans, although the chief had committed raids and robberies as early as 1859.

But the intensity of Cochise's warfare grew exponentially after Apache Pass. That summer, he killed as many Americans as he could find, all of them innocent, many hung upside down by their heels over a slow fire.

His rage turned the southern portions of Arizona and New Mexico into a no-man's land of bleached bones and charred wagon remains, and it even included plans, ultimately unfulfilled, to wipe out Tucson and the mine settlement of Patagonia, then the only two populated towns in Arizona.

Later in 1861 at the start of the Civil War, when military authorities abandoned Fort Breckenridge and Fort Buchanan, and unprotected civilians began leaving the territory, Cochise believed his effort at extermination of Americans was the reason.

**KNOWN AS FELIX WARD AT THE TIME OF
HIS KIDNAPPING, MICKEY FREE GREW UP
AMONG APACHES AND BECAME AN ARMY SCOUT.**

A s for Cochise at Apache Pass, it's tempting to wonder whether the matter might have been brought to a different conclusion, if not for his burning anger. Even though he did not initiate the encounter, and he was tricked by Bascom, he did kill his hostages first, and left their remains where the Americans were certain to find them.

This, as he must have known, was his family's death sentence. Furthermore, killing the hostages ended any chance that the abducted boy, Felix Ward, might be returned to his family. Not long after Cochise's war ended, Felix Ward emerged in 1872 as Mickey Free, and became one of the most fierce and renowned Army scouts in the Apache Wars. He had been raised by the San Carlos Apaches as one of their own.

Bascom's behavior also was unimpressive, and made more so by the deceit in his official report.

Author Sweeney noted that the lieutenant never mentioned that Welch was killed by his own men, instead leaving the impression Apaches had done it. Bascom also led his superiors to believe he'd received Wallace's note on the 6th, when he didn't read it until the 8th, and he skipped over the loss of government mules as if it were a meaningless event for which he had no responsibility.

Even so, Bascom was commended by his superiors and awarded two promotions before his death in action against Confederate troops at Valverde, New Mexico, a year later.

What is most noteworthy about the Apache Pass disaster, however, was how much it foretold what was to come. Distinguishing features of the episode would show up again and again in American-Apache relations — duplicitousness, savagery, an inability of Americans to distinguish between various bands of Indians, and similarly, a willingness among the Indians to take revenge against any available American, regardless of culpability.

The final feature, it seems, was its inevitability. Bascom, the West Pointer, was dutifully performing his country's work, according to orders; and Cochise, the chief, was defending his family and his people. With each side behaving in a manner entirely sensible to them, the killing began in earnest.

CHAPTER THREE

The Death of Mangas Coloradas

*Geronimo, no stranger to malignant brutality,
called the chief's killing "perhaps the
greatest wrong ever done to the Indians."*

———◆———

NEARLY A CENTURY AND A HALF AFTER THE FACT, THE STORY OF
the death of Chiricahua Apache Chief Mangas Coloradas
can be told with remarkable clarity. Eyewitness Daniel
Ellis Conner, with good use of detail in two separate versions,
described what he saw that night in January 1863. Other participants have filled in holes, providing answers to all the big
questions of fact.

Such honesty is unusual for people involved in what
plainly was murder.

Mangas, the equal of Cochise as a chief and leader of his
people, was lured by treachery to a meeting with a group of
miners. Then he was taken from the miners by the U.S. Army,
prodded like an animal with scorching-hot bayonets, and, when
he objected, shot to death.

Some partisans of the Chiricahua Apache band, noting
the almost total lack of remorse among the men present when
Mangas died, suggest that this was evidence of the soldiers'
inhumanity.

But it could also be seen as evidence of the enormous
fear they felt in the heart of Apache country, of how little they
knew about their enemy, of the chaotic state of war that existed on the frontier on which they operated.

At bottom, the episode was a very human mix of ambition and hatred, ignorance, and righteous revenge. It also was

a defining moment in the Apache conflict, one that infected relations between the two sides for decades.

Geronimo, no stranger to malignant brutality, called the chief's killing "perhaps the greatest wrong ever done to the Indians."

At the time of his execution, Mangas was past 70, a widely known Apache leader. In his 1868 book, *Life Among The Apaches*, John C. Cremony called him "undoubtedly the most influential Apache who has existed for a century."

Those who knew Mangas described an extraordinary specimen between 6 feet and 6 feet 7 inches tall (depending on whose version is accurate), with an enormous head, hair reaching to his waist, an aquiline nose, and a wide mouth, which, in Conner's description, resembled "a slit cut in a melon, expressionless and brutal."

Cremony said the chief's powerful frame was "corded with iron-like sinews and muscles," and his small eyes were "exceedingly brilliant and flashing when under any excitement — although his outside demeanor was as imperturbable as brass."

Appearance surely played a part in Mangas's acquisition of power among the eastern Chiricahua people. But so did his fierceness as a warrior.

In his over-heated style, Cremony commented on that, too, saying that Mangas's many and terrible raids made his name "the tocsin of terror and dismay throughout a vast region of country.

"He combined many attributes of real greatness with the ferocity and brutality of the most savage savage," continued Cremony, who knew the chief personally. "I dismiss him with disgust and loathing, not unmingled with some degree of respect for his abilities."

Historians have called Cremony's remarks baseless, at least as they describe Mangas's behavior toward whites, whom he trusted. But like many Apaches, he did harbor an acute hatred for Mexicans, a long enmity that reverberated from one revenge killing to another.

In 1845, according to historian Dan Thrapp, raids by Mangas into Mexico were so frequent and brutal that Mexicans mobilized a 1,000-man force to campaign against him. However, a revolution in their own country kept them from setting out.

Seven years later, John Greiner, acting superintendent of Indian Affairs in New Mexico, met Mangas at Acoma pueblo and asked him the reason for his hatred of Mexicans.

"I will tell you," the chief said. "Some time ago my people were invited to a feast; *aguardiente* or whiskey, was there. My people drank and became intoxicated and were lying asleep when a party of Mexicans came and beat out their brains with clubs.

"At another time a trader was sent among us from Chihuahua. While innocently engaged in trading . . . a cannon concealed behind the goods was fired upon my people, and quite a number were killed . . . How can we make peace with such people?"

The attack involving a cannon referred to scalp hunter John Johnson's 1837 massacre of Chief Juan Jose Compa and members of his band, at which Mangas might have been present.

Another formative incident — recorded only by Cremony but called apocryphal by Sweeney — occurred at Piños Altos, near present-day Silver City in southwestern New Mexico, a few miles from the site where Compa and members of his band were killed.

A gold rush in 1860 brought hordes of Americans to the area, Mangas's homeland. Troubled by the influx, Mangas offered to guide the miners to rich gold deposits in Mexico. But the miners, believing he only wished to lure them to ambush, turned the tables and captured the chief.

They roped him to a tree and whipped him. One observer said he was given "a dose of strap oil, well supplied by lusty arms."

This incident, if it occurred, helped convince Mangas that survival in a land of increasing white settlement required alliance with other Apache bands, possibly even Navajos.

To accomplish this, he married three of his daughters to

other powerful Indians, leading some to conclude that he possessed an unusual and statesmanlike intelligence. These unions, in Thrapp's words, "extended his influence and bound hundreds of the bravest and most resolute warriors to his standard."

The most significant such marriage was that of Mangas's daughter to Cochise, the powerful Chiricahua Apache chief 20 years his junior.

On July 15, 1862, the two joined forces at Apache Pass to ambush 122 Union soldiers under Capt. Thomas Roberts. The men were an advance column of California Volunteers, led by Gen. James H. Carleton, enroute to Santa Fe to take command of the Department of New Mexico. Carleton was under orders to rout Confederate troops in the region. The Rebels quickly pulled out, allowing Carleton to address the problem of Cochise's Apaches. Ever since 1861 and the withdrawal from the territory of federal troops to fight in the Civil War, his raiders had been killing every white man they came across.

As much as Cochise and Mangas wanted the blood of the troopers at Apache Pass, they were unprepared for the weapons brought against them. After regrouping his command following the initial volleys, Roberts and his men rolled out two 12-pound cannons, eventually routing the Indians and leaving an unknown number dead and wounded.

But the shooting wasn't over. Roberts sent a seven-man detachment back to Carleton's supply train, 13 miles west, to notify him of the ambush. These men also were attacked, and several separated from the main group.

One of them was John Teal. In his diary, he described the Indians closing in on him, and Teal focusing his fire on an old chief armed with a rifle. "But [he] was unwilling to fire at me without a rest.

"He had got to a bunch of gaita grass & was laying on his belly on the opposite side of the bunch with his rifle resting on the bunch pointed strait at me, which caused me to drop from the horse on the ground & the Indian shot the horse instead of me.

"The horse left & I laid low sending a bullet at them when-

GEN. JAMES HENRY CARLETON COMMANDED CALIFORNIA VOLUNTEERS ON THE WESTERN FRONT DURING THE CIVIL WAR.

ever I had a chance. We kept firing till it was dark when a lucky shot from me sent the chief off in the arms of his Indians."

The chief was Mangas. He was taken to a doctor in Janos, Mexico, 120 miles south, the Indians promising to wipe out the village if their chief died. The doctor apparently performed his job well.

Within a month, Mangas was back in the region of Piños Altos, a changed man now seeking peace. But that desire was thwarted by his reputation, which, with the exception of the previous 21 months, was earned primarily through depredations against Mexicans.

His view toward whites, according to Edwin Sweeney, author of the 1998 biography, *Mangas Coloradas: Chief of the Chiricahua Apaches*, was one of accommodation and diplomacy.

That wouldn't work for General Carleton, however, a stern New Englander who held to whatever he believed with a Puritan heat. In Cremony's view, he was a man of "unscrupulous ambition and exclusive selfishness" who thought he understood Apaches, but did not.

If Carleton had any initial sympathy for the Indians, it vanished as his command continued east after the fight at Apache Pass.

**BUILT IN 1856, THE ROAD THROUGH APACHE PASS SERVED
AS A STRATEGIC CORRIDOR BETWEEN FORT YUMA,
ON THE COLORADO RIVER, AND FORT THORN, NEW MEXICO.**

"As he marched along the Overland Mail Route east toward the Rio Grande," wrote Sweeney, "skeletons, skulls, graves and charred wagons marred the landscape, all stark testimonials to the audacity and brutality of the Indians."

By October 1862, Carleton was well aware of Mangas's stated desire for peace. But the general, lacking faith in the chief's word and outraged at the attack on his troops, ordered Gen. Joseph R. West, commander of the District of Arizona, to rout Mangas and his followers.

"The campaign to be made must be a vigorous one, and the punishment of that band of murderers and others must be thorough and sharp," Carleton told West.

In January 1863, Joseph Reddeford Walker and a party of 33 gold seekers arrived at old Fort McLane, then abandoned, about 20 miles southeast of Piños Altos. Their nerves were on edge due to constant Apache surveillance, and thus they were pleased when an advance guard of West's force, under Capt.

E.D. Shirland, arrived at the same place. By that time, Walker and his men had concluded that the only way to guarantee safe passage over Burro Mountain and on to the Pacific was to take a prominent Apache hostage. They settled on Mangas.

The kidnapping party traveled to Piños Altos and camped there. In his second account (the first was a letter to an Arizona historian), published in 1956 and titled *Joseph Reddeford Walker and the Arizona Adventure*, Conner wrote that the men drew the Indians to them by hoisting a white flag. For a time they negotiated at a distance in broken Spanish, then Mangas and three or four followers approached.

"Our men now presented their guns and ordered Mangas to stand still and surrender, which he did in surprise," Conner said. The warriors accompanying the chief were turned loose and Mangas was told that he, too, would be freed as soon as the gold party made it over the mountain.

The men got back to the fort, just as General West arrived with the main column of soldiers.

"The general walked out to where Mangas was in custody to see him and looked like a pygmy beside the old chief, who also towered above everybody about him in stature," according to Conner. "He looked careworn and refused to talk and evidently felt that he had made a great mistake in trusting the paleface on this occasion."

Next morning, West snatched the prized prisoner from the Walker group, and informed the chief he would remain in the custody of the United States for the rest of his life.

But West told his guards something entirely different, according to Pvt. Clark Stocking, who claimed to have overheard the general's orders:

"Men, that old murderer has got away from every soldier command and has left a trail of blood for 500 miles on the old stage line. I want him dead or alive tomorrow morning, do you understand? I want him dead."

That night, January 18, was cold, disagreeable and exceedingly dark. Mangas lay on the ground under sentry beside the soldiers' campfire, covered in a blanket. Conner, standing guard over the adjacent Walker camp, was close enough to see the sentries in the flicker of the firelight.

"I noticed that the soldiers were annoying Mangas in some way," he said, "and they would become quiet and silent when I was about approaching the fire, and kept so until I again walked off in the dark . . ."

Conner got close enough to witness what was happening:

"I could see them plainly by the firelight as they were engaged in heating their fixed bayonets in the fire and putting them to the feet and naked legs of Mangas, who was from time to time trying to shield his naked limbs from the hot steel. . . . I didn't appreciate this conduct one particle, but said nothing to them at the time and really I had some curiosity to see to what extent they would indulge in it.

"I was surprised at their ultimate intentions just before midnight when I was about midway of my beat and approaching the firelight.

"Just then Mangas raised himself upon his left elbow and began to expostulate in a vigorous way by telling the sentinels in Spanish that he was no child to be played with. But his expostulations were cut short, for he had hardly begun his exclamation when both sentinels promptly brought down their minnie muskets to bear on him and fired, nearly at the same time through his body."

Conner said these two guards each fired two more shots at Mangas. According to another account, a third soldier rushed up and shot the chief in the head with a pistol.

When Sgt. Henry Foljaine informed West of the shooting, the general asked, "Is he dead?"

"Yes, sir," was the response.

"Very well, Sergeant, then let his guards go to sleep."

The following morning, a soldier borrowed the camp cook's knife and scalped Mangas, then the body was dumped in a gully and crudely covered.

Days later, soldiers dug up the corpse, removed the head and boiled it in a pot in preparation for shipment to a museum in New York.

Phrenologist Orson Squire Fowler eventually examined Mangas's skull and declared its capacity greater than Daniel Webster's.

History records little outrage at Mangas's killing from soldiers of the California Column, or from settlers. The silence was resounding testimony to the state of the frontier in those years.

As for West's report to Carleton on Mangas's death, it resembles a work of fiction. He states that the chief died while trying to escape and that he, West, did everything possible to protect the prisoner.

"I have thus dwelt at length upon this matter in order to show that even with a murderous Indian, whose life is clearly forfeited by all laws, either human or divine, wherever found, the good faith of the U.S. military authorities was in no way compromised."

Most who have written of Walker's and the military's actions have done so, justifiably, in condemnation. But there is another side. Author Lee Myers presented it in the *New Mexico Historical Review* in 1966.

He argues that the Southwestern frontier at Carleton's arrival was defenseless and in chaos from Cochise's relentless war of revenge following the Bascom trouble. Moreover, the government in Washington was in desperate straits, losing battles to Confederate forces in the east, and at the same time trying to quell Apaches in the West.

Both these factors influenced Carleton, who probably viewed the killing as his duty, an act of pre-emptive self-defense against the marauding Apaches.

A nd if Carleton's view of Indians hardened as he saw the devastation they wrought, so did Walker's. Conner related an incident shortly before Mangas was killed, when the Walker party found three white men, victims of Apaches, "hanging by their ankles all in a row to a horizontal piñon limb" near Stein's Peak.

"Their hands were tied behind them and their heads hung to within a foot of the ground and a little fire had been built under each head," Conner said. "They were dead and the skin and hair had burned off of their skulls, giving them a ghastly appearance as they swung there perfectly naked."

In his *Historical Review* article, Myers responds to this with a striking remark: "Before we shed too many tears over the brutality of the military, it would be well to remember that they at least waited until the chief was dead before they cooked his head."

Carleton's critics often say he followed a policy of extermination toward Apaches, but so did Cochise toward whites. In the middle, between these two practitioners of total war, was Mangas, who paid with his life.

The effect of the chief's death, particularly the mutilation of his body, cannot be overstated. Sweeney, an eloquent and sympathetic chronicler of the Apache story, wrote that West's decision to execute Mangas failed to either defeat or mollify the Chiricahua — and in fact had the opposite effect, leading to 23 years of war.

"The ignominious circumstances surrounding his death," wrote Sweeney, "had compelled his people to continue fighting for a cause that he [Mangas] had realized was hopeless."

As Chiricahua warrior Asa Daklugie was quoted: "To an Apache the mutilation of the body is much worse than death because the body must travel through eternity in mutilated condition. Little did the White Eyes know what they were starting when they mutilated Mangas Coloradas."

CHAPTER FOUR

Eskiminzin's Revenge

By killing Charles McKinney, his friend,
Chief Eskiminzin committed a stunning betrayal.
Later, he explained: "I did it to teach my people
that there must be no friendship between them
and the white man. Anyone can kill an enemy,
but it takes a strong man to kill a friend."

———◇———

A FTER THE KILLING OF CHIEF MANGAS COLORADAS IN 1863, the war continued, marked by periods of relative calm followed by incidents of plunder and killing, and then the inevitable revenge. One of the most fascinating of such episodes occurred in southeastern Arizona in a modest San Pedro River farmhouse the first week in June 1871.

After dinner, over coffee, rolled cigarettes, and pleasant talk, an Aravaipa Apache chief suddenly drew his pistol and fired at eyeball range, killing a 35-year-old Irishman named Charles McKinney.

In the larger picture, the murder of an unknown farmer, sublimely cold though it was, hardly seems worthy of mention. But the event spoke volumes about the desperate times in which it occurred.

The killing was an outgrowth of the massacre a month earlier of at least 100 Aravaipa Apaches by a vigilante mob. The leader of the slaughtered band was Eskiminzin, who later said he pulled the trigger on McKinney to teach his people a hard lesson about never trusting whites.

But McKinney had nothing to do with the so-called Camp Grant Massacre. In fact, numerous sources report that the sim-

CHIEF ESKIMINZIN, WITH TWO OF HIS CHILDREN.

ple farmer had been a friend of the chief's to the instant of his death. By killing him, Eskiminzin committed one of the most stunning betrayals of this or any war.

The lead-up to McKinney's murder began in February 1871 when five Apache women approached Camp Grant, a hundred or so miles northeast of Tucson. They wanted help searching for the son of one of them who had been taken prisoner in the Salt River area of central Arizona.

    Their arrival at the military post came at a time of much hostility. Raids by Cochise's band, among others, had inflamed Arizona citizens against all Indians and furthered cries for the military to stop them. Whether the tribes were herded onto reservations or exterminated mattered little to the increasing numbers of settlers.

Amid this climate, Camp Grant's commander, Lt. Royal Whitman, treated the five visitors with unexpected kindness. Within days, more Apaches came to the camp to trade for badly needed clothing. Soon, at Whitman's encouragement, some 25 Apaches, including three chiefs, came to the post to talk. They were hungry, sick, and worn out from harassment by soldiers.

One of them, Eskiminzin, told Whitman that he wished his small band could live in peace in their homeland along Aravaipa Creek, not far from Camp Grant. The 37-year-old Maine-born lieutenant, knowing a reservation would soon be established in the White Mountains, tried to convince Eskiminzin to move his people there. But the chief refused.

"That is not our country, neither are they our people," Eskiminzin said. "Our fathers and their fathers before them have lived in these mountains and have raised corn in this valley. We are taught to make mescal, our principle article of food, and in summer and winter here we have a never-failing supply. At the White Mountains there is none, and without it we get sick."

The chief was told by Whitman that he would wire Arizona's military commander, Gen. George Stoneman, asking for permission to grant Eskiminzin's request. Meanwhile, if the chief brought his people to the post, Whitman would care for them as long as they remained peaceful. Whitman had to wait six weeks to hear from Stoneman, and the response to this important matter was mind-boggling. A clerk wrote to inform the lieutenant that he could not forward the memo to the general because it failed to include a note summarizing its contents, per Army instructions.

A timely response probably wouldn't have headed off the disaster to come. However, with Apache raids continuing south of the Gila River, the delay certainly didn't help.

Meanwhile, Apaches continued streaming into Camp Grant. By early April they numbered more than 400.

Impatient and fearful, the residents of Tucson reached the limit of their endurance after a raid on April 10 on the San Xavier Mission outside town and another one a few days later near the San Pedro River in which four settlers were killed.

Angry citizens led by William Sanders Oury, a participant in the Bascom Affair (see Chapter Two), and Jesus Maria Elias, a leader of the town's Mexican-descent population, formed a posse consisting of six Anglos, 92 Papagos, and 42 Mexicans to punish those responsible.

The mob set out after the killers, and believed it had found the raiders' trail along the San Pedro River northeast of Tucson. By then, Eskiminzin's band had moved, with Whitman's permission, five miles from the post to an area along Aravaipa Creek, where water was plentiful. Aravaipa Creek lies in a valley just east of the San Pedro.

Early on the morning of April 30, the vigilantes descended on Eskiminzin's rancheria (a term commonly used in the 19th century to refer to Indian camps) in what can only be described as mass murder. At least 100 Aravaipas died, many with their brains beaten out and their limbs hacked off. Some women, caught amid the fury, were raped and clubbed to death.

Oury described the action as if it were a great military victory, even though all but eight of the dead were women and children. Twenty-seven Apache youngsters were taken by the Papagos and sold into slavery in Mexico.

President Ulysses S. Grant called the massacre "purely murder," and historian Frank Lockwood described it as the "blackest page in the Anglo-Saxon records of Arizona."

Horrified by the brutality, Whitman tried to assure the Indians that soldiers were not responsible. He offered interpreters $100 apiece "to go to the mountains and communicate with them, and convince them that no officer or soldier of the United States Government had been concerned in the vile transaction."

When none accepted his offer, Whitman went to the scene and personally led a burial detail, aware that others of the band likely were watching from the surrounding hills.

"I thought the act of caring for their dead would be an evidence to them of our sympathy at least," he wrote, "and the conjecture proved correct, for while at the work many of them came to the spot and indulged in their expressions of grief, too wild and terrible to be described."

Eskiminzin, who probably was present that terrible morning, although that is uncertain, lost two wives and five children in the attack. By one estimate, 50 of his relatives were killed.

A few days after the massacre, Eskiminzin returned to Camp Grant carrying his only surviving daughter, Chita (sometimes referred to as Deenah) in his arms. He pleaded with Whitman for help in securing the return of the stolen children. The lieutenant vowed to do what he could, and convinced the chief not to go to war.

Hopes for peace ended in a tragic blunder about June 2. A scouting party from Camp Apache rode into Aravaipa Canyon and stumbled upon some Apaches, including Eskiminzin. In surprise and fear, the cavalry opened fire. No one was killed, but the chief finally had had enough.

"I have tried and my people have tried," he told Whitman. "But the peace you have promised to the Aravaipa has been broken, not one, but two times. Both times it was the Americans who broke the peace. The first one who breaks the peace is the one to blame."

Eskiminzin angrily departed for the mountains, killing McKinney on the way, his first act of retaliation. On July 13, he attacked a wagon train en route from Tucson's Camp Lowell to Camp Bowie, killing one soldier, although the chief lost 13 of his warriors and was himself wounded.

In September, Whitman sent word to Eskiminzin, still hiding in the mountains, that Vincent Colyer, a peace emissary sent by President Grant, was coming to the territory to establish a reservation for Apaches.

After meeting with White Mountain bands at Camp Apache early that month, Colyer went to Camp Grant and met with Eskiminzin on September 15, and again on September 17. Colyer told the chief he was creating a reservation for the band near Aravaipa Canyon and appointing Whitman as reservation agent.

However, peace again eluded Eskiminzin. On October 22, he was indicted by a federal grand jury for McKinney's murder. This caused the *Arizona Citizen*, which had been raging against Whitman and his peace plans, to intensify its editorial attacks.

On October 28, anti-Apache editor John Wasson sounded the trumpets against Eskiminzin: "Let the nation at large understand that an Indian chief of some note at the head of the peaceable and government-fed Indians at Camp Grant, did on or about June 1, 1871, unprovokedly kill Charles McKinney on his farm near Camp Grant."

The paper also chided Colyer for receiving "this same murdering chief," for clothing and feeding him at public expense, and for showing him high regard by putting "a showy sash on him."

Editor Wasson concluded: "Need any man be in doubt as to what impression was made upon that savage murderer's mind?"

The day before that editorial blast, deputy marshals departed Tucson for Camp Grant to arrest Eskiminzin. But he had been tipped — almost certainly by Whitman — that lawmen were coming and was gone by the time they arrived.

Adding to the outrage, the *Citizen* noted that, after the marshals left, Eskiminzin returned to the post and continued drawing regular rations.

A warrant for Eskiminzin's arrest never was served, even though his guilt was all but certain — in fact, admitted to by Eskiminzin, according to Jeanie Marion, author of an unpublished biography of the Aravaipa leader.

In his meetings with Colyer at Camp Grant, Eskiminzin said, "I was angry and killed the first white citizen. After that I wish to confess I went on a raid against the Papago to recover my children."

Author Marion said both these remarks are in Colyer's original handwritten report to the Secretary of the Interior, dated September 18. They were deleted from his final, published report.

"It's not clear who deleted them," Marion said in an interview. "I assume it was Colyer, but it's possible that someone in Washington did it. There was so much upset over the massacre, and officials in Washington really wanted to maintain peace as long as possible. If this came out, it wouldn't have presented Apaches in a good light."

Much later, Eskiminzin also admitted his guilt to Army scout Sam Bowman. In a quote that has echoed through the decades, he explained, "I did it to teach my people that there must be no friendship between them and the white man. Anyone can kill an enemy, but it takes a strong man to kill a friend."

Even with these confessions, the chief never was tried for the crime. He was saved, Marion maintained, by Colyer's sympathy and official Washington's desire to keep the lid on an inflammatory situation.

Oddly, though, Whitman, the peacemaker, was arrested and court-martialed for, as Wasson gleefully reported, being "deeply drunk, insulting women in public," and behaving in such a manner that "no gentleman could associate with him without feeling deeply humiliated."

The trumped-up charges were eventually dismissed, but the action showed the attitude of the military and the citizenry toward anyone favoring peace.

Eskiminzin's murder of McKinney haunted the chief the remainder of his days, during which he was repeatedly harassed and accused of whatever crime could be conveniently laid at his door.

When John P. Clum arrived in Arizona in June of 1874 to begin his tenure as Indian agent at San Carlos, he found Eskiminzin at new Camp Grant wearing shackles as he made adobe bricks.

For a number of reasons, including leading his band and six others in an escape from the guardhouse there in January of 1874, he had fallen into disfavor with the post commander, who considered him a "bad Indian."

After his release later that summer, the chief joined Clum at San Carlos, and for three years proved invaluable in helping manage the Apaches there. The two became close friends.

Eskiminzin departed San Carlos in 1877 and tried farming and ranching on the San Pedro River. The chief led a prosperous colony of six or eight families. He even had lines of credit, totaling several thousand dollars, with Tucson merchants, probably some of the same ones who had organized the massacre of his family.

But trouble was never far off. In 1887, while living peacefully as a rancher on the San Pedro River, Eskiminzin found himself in a dispute with the Pinal County sheriff over cattle supposedly rustled by one of his band.

The chief refused to surrender any of his men, no doubt believing they would be murdered, yet he still made honest efforts to resolve the matter. Nevertheless, the confrontation escalated until Eskiminzin had no choice but to move with his men to San Carlos to avoid arrest. Assuming his women and children were safe, he left them behind.

In his absence, a mob of 35, part of the sheriff's posse, trashed his ranch and took it over. "They came the next day after I left my ranch," Eskiminzin told Clum, "and they shot at my women, putting bullets through skirts, and drove them off."

In 1891, while living at San Carlos, the chief was arrested and accused — with scant evidence — of abetting the Apache Kid, a murderer and relative of the chief's, who had fled the reservation four years earlier.

Clum, Eskiminzin's passionate defender, wrote that without trial, and without the benefit of a single witness to his supposed wrongdoing, the chief was sent "as a military precaution" to Mount Vernon, Alabama, home to other imprisoned Apaches.

When Clum, founder of the *Tombstone Epitaph*, reunited with Eskiminzin in 1894, he asked the chief why he was at Mount Vernon. After stuttering furiously — Eskiminzin's habit when excited — he said, "Great lies! You know!"

The remark was a fitting summation of his dealing with the white eyes.

INDIAN AGENT JOHN CLUM CHAMPIONED ESKIMINZIN'S CAUSE AND LATER BECAME EDITOR OF THE *TOMBSTONE EPITAPH*.

Eskiminzin and his Aravaipas were finally released from Mount Vernon in 1894 and sent back to San Carlos, the only Apache band allowed to return to Arizona. They did so quietly and amid tight security, fearing an assassination attempt.

Death took Eskiminzin before the territory's citizens could. In December 1895, the Aravaipa chief died of chronic stomach trouble, at about age 67, without ever standing before a bar of justice for murdering Charles McKinney.

Whether he should have is a debate without resolution. Clum, at the very least, believed his action had to be judged in context. In a letter to the Indian Rights Association pleading for Eskiminzin's release from Mount Vernon, he wrote:

"Is it not strange that we can pass lightly over the 128

treacherous and cowardly murders instigated by white men [Camp Grant], while we carefully treasure the memory of a single killing by an Indian, and — after a lapse of 23 years — point to him and say, 'This man murdered his friend' — without even giving him the benefit of the circumstances which instigated the crime?"

Vincent Colyer, based on a letter to his superiors in Washington, plainly believed the answer was no. He said the massacre of Eskiminzin's family and people opened a condition of war between whites and Apaches, and Eskiminzin's killing of McKinney was "an incident in that war."

Also, Colyer wrote that losing so many members of his family at Camp Grant "seems to have practically crazed him."

Certainly the vigilantes responsible for the massacre were not held to answer, except by a five-day show trial that ended in acquittal after 19 minutes of deliberation. And it is highly likely the Aravaipas had not committed the raids for which they were blamed.

Author Marion said most historians believe the culprit was probably the band led by Chiricahua Chief Juh. "He was raiding out of Mexico at that time, but the military in Tucson wasn't aware of it and attributed it to the Aravaipas," said Marion. "But it's impossible to say with certainty who it was."

Historian Dan Thrapp contended that Eskiminzin's people were merely convenient targets, "the easiest collection of Apaches to kill."

So, Eskiminzin maintained he killed a friend to teach his people about the treachery of whites. It was the best way he knew to protect his people.

As impenetrable as the logic might be today, it said much about the power of rage and revenge in a time of war between two opposite cultures.

CHAPTER FIVE

End of the Line at Wickenburg and Retaliation at Date Creek

The melee at Camp Date Creek in September 1872 was a double cross within a double cross, and it almost cost George Crook, the man considered the greatest Indian fighter, his life.

———◆———

BLOODSHED AGAIN ROCKED ARIZONA TERRITORY IN NOVEMBER 1871 when Yavapai Indians killed six whites on a stagecoach west of Wickenburg.

The murders dashed hopes for peace and taught officials in Washington a hard reality about the white-Indian situation in Arizona — namely, that the fighting would end only when roving renegade bands were defeated in battle. The massacre also unleashed on renegade Apaches the man considered the greatest Indian fighter, George Crook.

His patience, intelligence, determination, and bravery would lead the way in the subjugation of the Indians. However, this man of character also was capable of duplicity, as those guilty of the so-called Wickenburg massacre learned when he lured them to a conference under the pretext of providing them with rations, all the while intending to spring a trap and arrest them.

But his plan nearly backfired when the Yavapais — identified in contemporary accounts as Apache-Mohaves — tried to turn the tables and assassinate the general. The melee at Camp Date Creek in September 1872 was a double cross within a double cross, and it almost cost Crook his life.

53

Crook became Arizona's new military leader in June 1871. At the time a lieutenant colonel, he arrived in a manner befitting his personality, "without baggage and without fuss," reports Frank Lockwood, in his book *The Apache Indians*.

"Not even the stage driver knew who this lean, quiet, muscular passenger was," wrote Lockwood. "He took up his task as unobtrusively as a Pinkerton detective."

Before darkness on the day he reached Tucson, Crook ordered officers in his southern command to report to him at once. He wanted to pick their brains for every bit of information about the Indian troubles.

His habit was to listen intently for long periods, but give no inkling of his own views. Many found his silence strange. But it compelled men to talk, revealing information they otherwise would have held tightly.

In early July, he undertook a reconnaissance of 675 miles, marching with five companies of cavalry and 50 Mexican scouts from Camp Bowie to Camp Apache, then on to Camp Verde and finally to Fort Whipple in Prescott.

His purpose, in addition to engaging whatever hostiles he came across, was to survey the landscape and come to know his troops. He also met with Indian leaders to encourage them to move onto government reservations, their past depredations forgotten, or be hunted down and killed.

With that work done, he turned his attention to fighting. He headed south again to engage the Yavapais, and the Tonto Apaches, an incorrigible band that raided and killed below the Mogollon Rim.

But he was stopped when President Grant, still believing peace was possible, sent to Arizona Territory the Secretary of the Permanent Board of Peace Commissioners, a quixotic group formed a few years earlier to advocate for the humane treatment of Indians.

Vincent Colyer arrived in August of 1871 and soon began a two-month tour of the territory to meet with Indian leaders. From his first appearance, this former abolitionist and prac-

GEORGE CROOK, THEN A LIEUTENANT COLONEL, ASSUMED
COMMAND OF THE DEPARTMENT OF ARIZONA IN 1871.

ticing Quaker drew howls of protest from citizens and newspapers fed up with the pretty theories of Eastern "peace fanatics," as some called them.

The strongest voice was that of John Marion, editor of the *Arizona Miner* of Prescott. Among other slanders, he referred to Colyer as a "cowardly, thieving Quaker and a red-handed assassin."

Arizona's military men resented Colyer as well. In his unpublished diary, John Gregory Bourke, Crook's aide, referred to him as "that spawn of hell," and Crook, in his autobiography, said the Indians, after assuring Colyer of their love for peace, followed behind him leaving "a trail of blood . . . from the murdered citizens."

The New York pacifist, though unpopular in some circles, was successful in convincing about 4,000 Apaches to move onto reservations. And Colyer's suggestion concerning Camp Date Creek, 65 miles southwest of Prescott, proved eerily prescient.

According to Sidney Brinckerhoff, author of an extensive history of the Date Creek military outpost, Colyer was worried about the Indians loitering there. He wanted them removed to Camp Verde, but Crook preferred they be left at Date Creek until spring.

As a result, noted Brinckerhoff in the fall 1964 edition of *The Smoke Signal*, a publication of the Tucson Corral of the Westerners, Crook declared a temporary reservation at Date Creek and authorized rations for the Yavapais.

Brinckerhoff said the Indians were subject to little control if they kept the peace. But some bands slipped away to raid passing wagons trains and ranches, then retreated to the protection of the post.

In truth, Colyer's peacemaking efforts were less than successful. Lockwood reports that within a year of his entry into the territory, Indians had made about 50 raids and killed more than 40 citizens.

No reservation and no combination of high-minded words could loose the bands of warriors from their raiding ways. Sooner or later they would strike. It turned out to be sooner, and ironically enough, the raid proved Colyer correct in his concerns about Date Creek.

On November 5, 1871, a week after Colyer landed back in Washington, Indians attacked a westbound stage as it dipped into a wash eight miles west of Wickenburg.

Prescott's *Miner* reported that the eight people on board "were assailed, from every side, by showers of bullets." Those who came on the scene later found 17 slug holes in the coach.

The brutal raid shocked the nation and received page-one notice in *The New York Times*. Among the dead were three members of a prestigious government survey party, including Frederick Loring, a 22-year-old Harvard-trained journalist who was rapidly gaining a national reputation.

William Kruger and Mollie Sheppard, the only survivors, fled west into the desert, where they met a mail wagon from Ehrenberg.

In spite of initial suspicions that whites or Mexican bandits had committed the deed, military authorities believed the killers were Indians. But Crook needed proof, and in his patient and methodical fashion, went to work to learn the identities of the guilty.

End of the Line at Wickenburg and Retaliation at Date Creek

MEMOIRIST JOHN GREGORY BOURKE, SEATED LEFT,
WITH GENERAL CROOK AND AN UNIDENTIFIED OFFICER,
RECORDED FIRST-HAND IMPRESSIONS OF THE APACHE WARS.

The *Miner* reported that in January 1872, rancher William Gilson informed the general that he had good reason to believe Date Creek Indians were mixed up in the affair. Crook responded by dispatching spies, both Indian and white, to find evidence.

A big break came when a Yavapai boy, who'd been raised by scout Dan O'Leary, told O'Leary he'd been summoned by the perpetrators to help them determine the denomination of the greenbacks they'd taken at the time of the massacre. The information was relayed to Crook.

The general was also helped by the friendly Mohave chief, Irataba. He informed Crook that the murderers, after returning to Date Creek, went to Irataba's reservation on the Colorado River, boasted of what they'd done, and spent the greenbacks and other plunder.

Now confident of the killers' identities, Crook, as noted in his official report, used great care to maintain secrecy while "getting the Indians into position so as to capture them."

In March 1872, he rode out of Fort Whipple, accompanied by Bourke and another lieutenant named Ross. Crook told no one of his destination as he headed west on the Mohave

Road toward the Colorado River.

Crook's party stopped at Beale Springs, near present-day Kingman, and convinced friendly Wallapais (the present-day spelling is Hualapais) to help persuade the Yavapais to come to Date Creek, where they'd be fed and cared for by the government.

But Crook's true desire was to arrest the guilty. He was on his way to do so when, for the second time, he received orders to stop. The peace commissioners wanted to try again.

Washington's latest emissary was Oliver Otis Howard, a one-armed, bible-thumping brigadier general. Through the spring and summer of 1872, he did as Colyer had done — talked with Indians, made adjustments to the reservation system and generally aggravated Crook to no end with his self-perceived mission as Moses to the Indians.

And like Colyer, his efforts, while laudatory in theory, could not silence the rifles.

By early September, 1872, Howard was gone and Crook was ready, again, to fight. As Crook wrote in his autobiography, he wanted the first act in that campaign to be the capture of the Yavapais responsible for the Wickenburg massacre.

But his mission had become significantly more complicated.

In his 1896 book *On The Border With Crook*, Bourke said word had reached the general, through friendly Wallapais, that "when he next visited Camp Date Creek, he was to be murdered with all those who might accompany him."

The Yavapais were plotting to appear outside Crook's quarters at the post and inform him of their desire to talk. When the general made his appearance, the Indians were to sit in a semi-circle in front of the door, each with his carbine under his blanket, or carelessly exposed on his lap.

After a pleasant talk, the leading conspirator would request tobacco, then roll a cigarette. At the first puff, the Indian next to the chief would raise his carbine and shoot the general.

The tribe would then break from the reservation and head to the inaccessible cliffs and canyons at the head of the Santa

Maria fork of the Bill Williams River.

Bourke said the plot would have succeeded if Crook had not been warned, and if the commander at Date Creek had not unexpectedly died, leaving the post without an officer. The death caused Crook to rush there ahead of the expected time, before all the Yavapai conspirators could gather.

When Crook arrived at the post on September 7, he found that two-thirds of the Indians who should have been on the reservation had left. The following day the Yavapai chief Ochocama — wanted by Crook for the murder, in 1866, of the territory's Superintendent of Indian Affairs — returned with 50 warriors.

A raiding party from this band, part of the larger reservation population of close to 1,000, had committed the Wickenburg killings.

In a letter to his superiors after the episode, Crook said the Date Creek Indians were "uneasy and suspicious, and in very bad temper, appearing with their arms and war paint."

The groups met on the parade grounds. With the general were Bourke; Ross; Lt. William Volkmer; some civilians; and a dozen packers, who according to Bourke, strolled carelessly forward.

But each was "armed to the teeth, and every revolver was on the full cock, and every knife ready for instant use."

Two principal accounts exist of what transpired next — one by Bourke, who was there, and the other by the *Miner*, published on September 28, 1872. The paper contradicted Bourke regarding which side used tobacco as a signal to begin the action.

In the newspaper's version, Crook and Irabata planned to have Mohaves hand tobacco to each of the guilty Yavapais, thus identifying them; then soldiers would arrest them.

The first to receive tobacco was Ochocama, who hung his head and didn't let on that he understood what the Mohaves meant.

"But he was persuaded to take hold of it," the *Miner* noted, "and while his countenance changed rapidly from one blue color to another, he finally dropped the tobacco."

After other guilty Indians were given theirs, a soldier

stepping forward to make an arrest was stabbed. He then drew his pistol and fired, after which, the paper said, "Indians and soldiers were cross-firing upon each other."

Bourke said the shooting started when one of the Indians, after asking for tobacco, rolled a cigarette and prepared to smoke. At this signal, another Yavapai raised his carbine and fired at Crook.

But in his letter, dated September 10, Crook seemed to confirm the newspaper's version. "As they were designated," he wrote, referring to the guilty, "the soldiers stepped up to arrest them when one of the Indian friends, standing back of the soldiers, stabbed one of them in the back."

However it happened, the action was swift. Bourke said the effort to kill Crook was thwarted by Ross, who struck the arm of the would-be murderer, deflecting his bullet. The shot killed the Indian standing behind Crook.

The Yavapai who gave the signal to fire, if it happened that way, found himself in the grip of packer Hank Hewitt. Bourke said Hewitt attempted to drag the Indian to the guardhouse, but instead grabbed the thrashing Yavapai by both ears and bashed his head against some rocks.

This, Bourke wrote, "either broke his skull or brought on concussion of the brain, as the Indian died that night in the guard-house."

The *Miner* reported that most of the Indians ran away when the firing commenced, but Ochocama and others "fought like demons."

So did Crook's packers. Scout O'Leary grabbed Ochocama by his long hair, wrestled him to the ground and tied him up, then led him to the guardhouse to join his brother, Te-Yee-Made-Yee. The latter had been imprisoned earlier for insubordination.

At 4 A.M. the morning of September 9, according to the post returns from Camp Date Creek, Ochocama and Te-Yee-Made-Yee attempted to escape, along with another Indian.

Ochocama was wounded, "severely, if not mortally," in the effort, although the nature of the wounds was not specified. The *Miner*, however, said he was shot twice and bayoneted, but still managed to escape into the hills. Te-Yee-Made-Yee was killed at the same time.

In all, seven Indians died in the struggle and others were wounded.

"Mr. Hewitt said many more could and would have been killed but for the earnest effort of" Crook and Dr. Herman Bendell, Arizona's Superintendent of Indian Affairs, reported the *Miner*.

In spite of the violence, which Crook regretted, he comported himself well, as Hewitt noted. But the general never mentioned in his report how close he came to death.

Even in his autobiography, Crook glossed over the danger, writing, "On the eighth day of September, 1872, in attempting to make the arrest, some of the Indians were killed, and some of our party narrowly escaped being shot."

Dan Thrapp, who wrote of the episode in his book, *Al Sieber: Chief of Scouts*, theorized the general's silence perhaps stemmed from the realization that his unorthodox method of selecting mostly civilians to execute the arrests "might be subject to censure."

After the fight, Crook encouraged the Indians to return to the reservation with a vow of amnesty, and marched against those who refused to come in. Late in September, a column of the 5th Cavalry, along with Wallapai scouts, fought the hostiles at the head of the Santa Maria, killing 40 and breaking their rebellion.

Crook's success resonated throughout the territory. The new commander had won the trust of his soldiers and the respect of his enemy. Just as important, the Wickenburg massacre and the fight at Date Creek helped turn the minds of eastern leaders to the necessity of war.

Free now to soldier, Crook set off on his campaign against the Yavapais and Tonto Apaches.

CHAPTER SIX

The Winter Campaign

"To polish a diamond there is nothing like its
own dust, and it is the same with these fellows
[Apaches]. Nothing breaks them up like turning
their own people against them." — George
Crook, explaining his use of Indian Scouts

L IEUTENANT COLONEL GEORGE CROOK'S OFFENSIVE, KNOWN
to history as the Winter Campaign, began November 16,
1872, with numerous small commands criss-crossing
much of Arizona's Apache Country. They swept over the Pinal,
Superstition, and Mazatzal mountain ranges; along the Mogollon
Rim; and down the Salt, Verde, and Black rivers. The soldiers'
aim was to drive whatever renegades they encountered toward
the Tonto Basin for a final cleanup.

The work was hard, bloody, and a major success. One
reason for the success was Crook's use of pack mules rather
than bulky supply wagons. This gave his forces great mobility
and speed in reaching previously inaccessible hideouts.

But his most important decision — for the outcome of
the campaign and the entire war — was using Indian scouts to
guide and fight with his troops. No single betrayal was more
pivotal than the willingness of thousands of Arizona's Indians,
especially Apaches, to turn against their own people in the
fight against the soldiers.

In organizing his scout companies — first from a mix of
tribes, later almost exclusively from Apache bands — Crook
took a big gamble. Few in the military, and even fewer among
the public, believed his daring idea would work. But he was
convinced there was no other way. Apaches were physically
and mentally tougher than white soldiers, better conditioned,

KNOWN TO APACHES AS THE GRAY FOX, GEORGE CROOK
PRACTICED THE MAXIM "THE BEST DEFENSE IS ATTACK."

and expert in their knowledge of Arizona's sometimes impassable terrain.

Crook also understood the social structure of the Apache
people. They were not a tribe in the traditional sense, but a
collection of bands bound by a common culture and often by
blood ties. Each was led by an independent chief whose band
was loyal only to him. Crook knew that long-standing rivalries
and hatreds existed between these bands and that he could ex-
ploit them to his benefit.

"To polish a diamond there is nothing like its own dust,
and it is the same with these fellows," he once said. "Nothing
breaks them up like turning their own people against them. . . .
It is not merely a question of catching them better with Indians,
but of a broader, more enduring aim . . . their disintegration."

Crook came quickly to his opinion about Indian scouts. During
his long reconnaissance march upon arriving in Arizona in
1871, he was accompanied by 50 Mexican scouts. He hired them
on the recommendation of Arizona Governor A.P.K. Safford, who
told Crook that with "a little pinole and dried beef," Mexicans
could travel the countryside without pack mules.

**GOVERNOR A.P.K. SAFFORD, GOVERNOR OF ARIZONA TERRITORY
AT THE TIME OF CROOK'S WINTER CAMPAIGN.**

"They could go inside an Apache and turn him wrong side out in no time at all," Safford told him.

But by the time he reached Camp Apache, Crook had soured on the Mexicans. As he wrote in his autobiography, "Here I refit, leaving my Mexican outfit, pinole and all, to be discharged."

He then embarked on long talks with Coyoteros and White Mountain Apaches to convince them to join him as scouts. John G. Bourke, a mililtary officer, was present at the councils and included a portion of Crook's reasoning in his book, *On The Border With Crook*:

> "If every one came in without necessitating a resort to bloodshed he should very glad; but, if any refused, then he should expect the good men to aid him in running down the bad ones.
>
> "That was the way the white people did it; if there were bad men in a certain neighborhood, all the law-abiding citizens turned out to assist the officers of the law in arresting and punishing those who would not behave themselves. He hoped that the Apaches would see that it was their duty to do the same."

At Camp Apache, Crook organized a small company of scouts

and returned to Verde to prepare his campaign. In this work, he was in constant conference with scouts and interpreters concerning, as Bourke said, "all that was to be done and all that was positively known of the whereabouts of the hostiles."

The commands began their march on November 16, 1872, each accompanied by a scout unit. It shortly became clear that Crook's soldiers would have foundered without them.

The scouts, not the soldiers, made most of the early contacts with the renegades. Bourke said they stayed between 12 and 24 hours ahead of the main command, "the intention being to make use of them to determine the whereabouts of the hostiles, but to let the soldiers do the work of cleaning them out."

But the scouts often opened the ball before the soldiers could catch up. "It was difficult to restrain the scouts, who were too fond of war to let slip any good excuse for a fight," wrote Bourke.

Their everyday value as trackers was immense. Mike Burns, himself an Apache, described an episode from the winter of 1872:

> "The soldiers passed right by a camp of Indians on a thick flat of cedar; it was snowing and the wind was blowing right into the soldiers' faces. They never looked down on the ground to see if there were any tracks of the Indians, and went right on by.
>
> They always had to have Indians to guide them and to fight the Apaches in their style, and also to find them water holes. Only for the aid of the Indians, the soldiers were worth nothing."

One of the most dramatic episodes of the offensive occurred in late December 1872. A scout named Nan-ta-je led the combined forces of Maj. William H. Brown and Capt. James Burns, some 220 soldiers, to Salt River Cave in the Mazatzal Mountains. He warned that the approach to the stronghold was so dangerous it would have to be done at night and that if discovered, they would likely all be killed.

**THE ENLISTMENT OF WHITE MOUNTAIN APACHE SCOUTS
TO TRACK WARRING INDIANS GAVE THE ARMY
ITS MOST EFFECTIVE WEAPON.**

But the soldiers successfully surrounded the cave, and at dawn on December 28, they began shooting, killing six Yavapai warriors as they danced before a fire inside. After this first volley, the scouts called on the Indians inside the cave to surrender.

"The only answer was a shriek of hatred and defiance," wrote Bourke, "threats of what we had to expect, yells of exultation at the thought that not one of us should ever see the light of another day, but should furnish a banquet for the crows and buzzards."

It was the other way around. Sharpshooters fired against the sloping rock walls, allowing their ricocheting bullets to kill Indians who had retreated back from the opening. Soldiers also rolled enormous boulders into the cave from a precipice above its entrance, loosing thunder and more death upon those inside.

An estimated 76 Yavapais died in the celebrated fight, and none of it would've been possible if not for Nan-ta-je, who supposedly grew up inside the cave.

Other engagements in the Winter Campaign were far smaller. But even when they weren't fighting, Crook's men did great damage, forcing the Apaches to keep moving through cold and blowing snow. Troops torched rancherias, destroyed food caches, and prevented the Indians from hunting for more.

"There was no spot on mountain or mesa or in deepest canyon where a hostile Indian could rest in safety," wrote historian Frank Lockwood.

The end came on April 6, 1873, when the Yavapai leader, Cha-Li-Pun, claiming to represent 2,300 Yavapais, surrendered at Fort Verde. He told Crook he was giving up because the white men "had too many copper cartridges."

"I want to be your friend," the chief said. "I want my women and children to be able to sleep at night, and to make fire to cook their food without bringing your troops down on us. We are not afraid of the Americans alone, but we cannot fight you and our own people together."

Crook, for his part, told Cha-Li-Pun the Indians who died did so from their own folly in not obeying his edict to come in. In one of the great quotes of the war, he explained, "There was nothing else to do but go out and kill them until they changed their minds."

The campaign drew universal praise, and Crook was saluted. But his troubles weren't over. He had to deal with several bands of renegades, mostly Tonto Apaches, still free in the wilds.

And his nemesis, the Yavapai band leader Delshay, whom Crook dubbed "the liar," would prove a persistent thorn. He surrendered on April 25, 1873, and was placed on the White Mountain Reservation. Shortly after, he bolted with his band

and made his way to Camp Verde, again promising to stay put.

But as Crook wrote, "the restraint on the reservation was irksome to his wild spirit, which was unused to any curbing.

"One day, without warning, he surrounded the white men at the agency. Lt. W.S. Schuyler was in charge, backed only by agency employees. Delshay would certainly have assassinated them all but for the interposition of the scouts, who compelled them to desist."

That night, Delshay and 40 of his followers ran to the mountains again. A short time later, on May 27, some 1,000 Indians, half of them armed and many in bad temper, gathered at the San Carlos Agency to collect rations. For reasons that remain unclear, Lt. Jacob Almy, a well-loved Quaker soldier, walked unarmed into the group, accompanied by six other soldiers, to arrest one of its most volatile members.

Suddenly a shot rang out and he was hit in the side. "Oh, my God!" he exclaimed. Then another bullet struck him in the head and Almy was dead. Amid shouting and chaos, the Indians ran in every direction. Some bolted the reservation and marauded through the San Pedro Valley, brutally murdering some families there. Most returned to the reservation before long to surrender, but an angry Crook refused to take them back, saying he'd just as soon drive them back into the mountains and kill them all.

"They begged to be allowed to remain," Crook wrote, "making all kinds of promises for the future. I finally compromised by letting them stay, provided they would bring in the heads of certain of the chiefs who were ringleaders, which they agreed to."

The named outlaws were Chuntz, Chan-Dei-Si and Co-Chi-Nay.

But in almost a year of fighting, during which Crook's men routed the followers of these renegade leaders, he was unable to kill the leaders themselves. That work was left to scouts seeking to collect Crook's reward.

In May of 1874, several scouts rode up to the parade ground in front of Crook's tent at San Carlos and dumped the severed head of Co-Chi-Nay into the dust. Within a few weeks, scouts brought Chan-Dei-Si's head to Camp Apache, "which

APACHE SCOUTS WHO TRACKED GERONIMO'S WAR PARTY
WORE BLACK COATS AND INDIVIDUALIZED HEAD GEAR.

leaves now only Chuntz's head on his shoulder," Crook noted.

But Crook was still thinking about Delshay, too. In a telegram
to Lt. Walter Schuyler, commander at Camp Verde, he wrote:
"Start your killers as soon as possible after the head of DelChe
& Co. The more prompt these heads are brought in, the less liable
other Indians, in the future, will be to jeopardize their heads."

Chuntz was the next to go. On July 25, his head, along
with the heads of six of his followers, were brought in to San
Carlos. Crook mounted all seven skulls on sticks and planted
them on the parade ground, a not-so-subtle message to the San
Carlos Apaches about the fate of killers.

The last of the group, Delshay, posed an interesting problem. At the end of July, two separate groups of Apache scouts
brought in heads, one to Verde and one to San Carlos, each
claiming they had killed Delshay.

"Being satisfied that both parties were earnest in their
beliefs," Crook wrote, "and the bringing in of an extra head
was not amiss, I paid both parties. This about quieted them,
but small parties would still sift out in the mountains."

As he departed his Arizona command in 1875, it appeared to Crook, by now a general, as if the Apaches had been defeated. He crowed that "his troops had terminated a campaign which had lasted from the days of Cortez."

That, of course, proved premature. But he and others involved in these early offensives saw up close the value of the scouts. Between 1872 and 1874, military units operating without scouts killed or captured fewer than 20 hostile Indians. But the scouts themselves killed 272 of their own people and brought in another 313 captives.

And the Apaches were the best of the best. "They were wilder and more suspicious than the Pimas and Maricopas," wrote Bourke, "but far more reliable, and endowed with a greater amount of courage and daring."

In the words of Lt. W.E. Shipp, 10th Cavalry, who fought renegade Apaches in Mexico later in the war, the Chiricahuas especially were a "never-ending source of wonder." In the *United States Cavalry Journal* in December 1892, he wrote, "Their knowledge of the country; their powers of observation and deduction; their watchfulness, endurance and ability to take care of themselves under all circumstances, made them seem at times superior beings from another world."

CHAPTER SEVEN

Deceit at Cibecue

Known to whites as the Prophet,
Nock-ay-det-klinne told his people the chiefs
would be raised [from the dead] only when
whites were driven from the country — and
it would happen when the corn was ripe.

———◆———

C APT. EDMUND HENTIG WAS SHOT IN THE BACK IN THE FIRST volley and died before his face struck the ground. His orderly, Pvt. Edward Livingstone, was hit by at least two bullets and died alongside Hentig. Then came the full roar of gunfire as chaos descended on Cibecue Creek.

Horses reared and bolted. Pack mules jumped crazily amid the whiz of bullets. From the brush along the creek bed, barely ten feet below the rise where the soldiers had camped, Apache riflemen shouted their shrill war cry.

One of the participants later said he had never heard the intense gunfire he did that Sunday afternoon, August 30, 1881.

When the fight ended, six soldiers lay dead and another would succumb hours later, the highest number of soldiers killed in any battle between the military and Indians in Arizona. Most lost their lives when 22 enlisted scouts turned their rifles on the Army command.

This stunning mutiny, six years after Gen. George Crook left Arizona, showed just how badly the territory's Indian situation had deteriorated since he left his command. Control of the reservations had diminished to a dangerous degree, and corruption had worked its way into the very fabric of the government's work.

Cibecue was the culmination of trouble long brewing. The

episode, fueled by the machinations of a powerful Apache mystic, was one of the least understood events of the Apache Wars. It has been studied through the distortions of politics and cultural perception for more than a hundred years, with little common understanding.

At the bottom of the Cibecue fiasco was Nock-ay-det-klinne, a slight, pale-skinned White Mountain Apache chief and medicine man who rose to extraordinary prominence as a spiritual leader of his people.

At some point, possibly through contact with Mormons in Arizona, he was introduced to the story of Jesus Christ. The medicine man became fascinated with the concept of the resurrection and began preaching a new religion known as *na-il-de*, to return from the dead.

By the summer of 1881, Nock-ay-det-klinne, known to whites as the Prophet, was holding what historian Dan Thrapp described as primitive, revival-type meetings at his camp on Cibecue Creek. His followers guzzled *tiswin*, a drink made of fermented corn, and danced until they collapsed.

"He dreamed his way into the subconscious of his people, arousing them to a fervor of devotion and trust," wrote Thrapp.

The fuse was lit when this strange figure promised to raise two Apache chiefs from the dead. Indians who had been to the medicine man's dances reported to military authorities that "the chiefs were partly out of their graves and resurrected to the knees," according to Charles Collins, author of *Apache Nightmare: The Battle at Cibecue Creek*.

The informants also said the chiefs were "visible to all Indians" and all that remained to complete the resurrections was for the medicine man's followers to bring him gifts of horses, saddles, blankets, cattle and food.

Many complied. But when the promised resurrections didn't take place, Collins believes, the medicine man invented a shrewd ruse to shift the energies of his people from his own failure to the white menace.

Nock-ay-det-klinne told his people the chiefs would be raised up only when whites were driven from the country — and it would happen when the corn was ripe.

"I think he was out to make a name for himself and to take from his people what he could get," said Collins in an interview. "But things spun out of control."

San Carlos Indian agent Joseph Tiffany, believing the dances excited "a great many foolish young warriors and bucks to the detriment of good order," summoned band leaders and tried to convince them they were being duped.

But the Apaches had fallen under Nock-ay-det-klinne's spell, including the scouts of Company A. Second Lt. Thomas Cruse, their commander at Fort Apache, said that when they returned from the dances, which they were given permission to attend, they were sullen, uncommunicative, and in Thrapp's words, "grumbling that this was Indians' country, not whites'."

At the beginning of August, when the medicine man's followers gathered north of Fort Apache, Cruse sent his right-hand man, Sam Bowman, to spy on them. But Bowman, part black, part Cherokee, and typically unafraid, returned to Fort Apache shaken at what he had witnessed. He astonished Cruse by refusing to talk to him about it, but to others he darkly predicted that trouble was coming.

What began as an internal Apache matter had turned into a military concern. What if the Prophet's many followers, excited by his promise of a return to the old ways, rose up and revolted?

In mid-August, Brevet Maj. Gen. Eugene Carr, commander of Fort Apache, received a telegram from Maj. Gen. Orlando Willcox, head of the Department of Arizona, ordering him to arrest Nock-ay-det-klinne.

But Carr wasn't sure he could trust the Indian scouts to help apprehend the medicine man. Cruse advised Carr that if trouble erupted among White Mountain Apaches, nearly all his Indian scouts would join the renegades. He recommended discharging them.

Carr wired Willcox, asking for permission to do so and to replace them with ones he trusted. But bad weather brought down the telegraph lines, and Carr never received Willcox's approval of that plan.

On his own, the Carr made up his mind to bring the scouts. He knew he couldn't find the medicine man without them and reasoned that leaving the scouts at Fort Apache, garrisoned by only 60 men, was even more risky.

On August 29, Carr left for Cibecue with 79 enlisted men and five officers of the 6th Cavalry, accompanied by 23 scouts. He had little idea of the danger he faced.

The command traveled 29 miles before making camp on Carrizo Creek that night. The following day, about 2 miles from Cibecue, the unit reached a fork in the Verde Trail. Cruse and his command, including the scouts, who had pulled ahead of Carr's group, turned left toward the thick brush along the creek. He did so at the recommendation of the scouts.

Carr sent word to Cruse to retrace his steps and take the shorter right fork instead. When Cruse obeyed the order and turned around, his scouts exhibited a good deal of anger.

Author Charles Collins noted that several officers later studied the matter and concluded that the scouts, in union with the Cibecue Apaches, had planned to ambush the command in the creek bottom.

"If their plot had worked, the number of soldiers killed would've been far greater," said Collins, the first researcher to unearth evidence of an ambush attempt.

When Carr arrived at Cibecue, he told Nock-ay-det-klinne of his intention to bring him back to the fort. The medicine man agreed, smiling through much of the discussion, including when Carr told him he would be killed if he tried to escape, or if any of his followers attempted a rescue.

Nock-ay-det-klinne's followers, many carrying carbines, shadowed Carr's men as they moved away from Cibecue. Two miles downstream, when the command stopped to make camp, Cruse knew that the much-feared explosion had arrived.

In an 1883 letter to a friend, he wrote: "On the way down [the creek] the Indians kept coming out from the adjacent bluffs and ravines, and when we reached the camping place there were about 200 armed Indians around us, and I felt as if I was standing on a can of dynamite with a quick fuse attached."

As the soldiers busied themselves unloading pack mules and setting up tents on the small rise above the creek, Carr ordered Hentig to remove the Indians from the vicinity of the camp.

He approached them, shouting, *"U-ka-she! U-ka-she!"* — meaning "get out" in Apache. At the same time, a highly excited Indian on horseback began yelling at both the scouts and the Cibecue Indians, as if giving orders.

In Collins' detailed reconstruction of the event, scout Dandy Jim walked between Hentig and the mounted Indian. The captain grabbed the scout's arm and said, *"U-ka-she!"*

When Dandy Jim responded that he was a soldier, Hentig said, "Well, if you are, go to camp," and shoved him back. Dandy Jim started walking behind Hentig, looking sideways at him as he went.

As this was going on, the mounted Indian drew a rifle from his saddle scabbard, waved it over his head, and gave the war cry. A soldier hollered, "Watch out! They're going to fire!"

Immediately, a volley came from the Cibecue Apaches. The scout Dead Shot said something to the other scouts, after which they raised their .45 caliber Springfield rifles and fired.

Eugene Condon, a blacksmith, saw Dandy Jim drop to one knee and shoot Captain Hentig in the back from about 15 feet. The captain's hands flew up, and he yelled, "Oh, my God!"

"It seemed as if lightning had struck," Cruse wrote of the fight's opening. "I was stunned for a moment, for I saw that our scouts had fired on us, then I didn't know whether I was shot or not, because they were not 20 feet from me. Then I saw that it was live or die right there, and as another volley came, I dropped to the ground and then got up and got my gun."

Amid the racket of battle, Carr ordered Sgt. John McDonald to kill the medicine man, who was crawling with his woman toward the scouts. The sergeant, though wounded himself, shot Nock-ay-det-klinne through both thighs.

Another soldier, trumpeter William Benites, seeing that Nock-ay-det-klinne still lived, pulled his pistol and tried to finish him with a bullet in the neck.

Amid the fighting, Carr lost track of his 15-year-old son, Clark, who, on vacation from school, accompanied his father on the mission. The general looked around in panic and called his name.

"Here I am!" came the response. "What do you want?" The boy was seated on the ground with his rifle, about 50 feet from the scouts.

"I think that Clarke [sic] was the only person in the whole command who got the slightest degree of enjoyment out of the whole fight," said Cruse. "He had a small Winchester .44 and had got to shoot it to his heart's content with none to say, 'Don't!'"

When the shooting stopped at nightfall, Carr buried his dead in a mass grave. Before leaving for Fort Apache, he ordered First Lt. William Carter to make sure Nock-ay-det-klinne was dead.

Remarkably, he wasn't. Carr's men then bashed in the Prophet's skull with their rifle butts.

One of the troopers, Thomas Foran, an Irish immigrant, died en route to the fort. His agony from a bullet through the bowels was so extreme that Assistant Surgeon George McCreery struggled to keep him in his saddle, even roping him in place.

Foran's eventual and blessed death occurred just as the command crested a hill. *Chicago Times* correspondent John Finerty, who interviewed Carr's troops after Cibecue, described Foran straightening in his saddle and saying:

> "'It's no use, doctor, I'll never live to get to the bottom of this.' He begged to be untied, and when his request was granted he suddenly sprang a yard into the air and fell at full length, perfectly dead."

The command reached Fort Apache at 3 o'clock on the afternoon of August 31. On September 4, the front page of *The New York Times* — under the headline, "Shot Down By Indians!" — reported that Carr, seven officers, and from 60 to 110 privates had been murdered by Apaches. Cruse cracked that "during the fall and winter we had the pleasure of reading our own obituary."

Apaches responded with fury to the death of their medicine man. Loose bands looted and murdered throughout the region, prompting the War Department to bring in additional troops to regain order. With the government promising a fair trial, several of the scouts of Company A turned themselves in at San Carlos.

Three of them — Dandy Jim, Dead Shot, and Skippy — were found guilty of desertion and murder, and they were executed at Fort Grant on March 3, 1882. Of the 23 members of Company A, only Mose, who was guarding Nock-ay-det-klinne, remained loyal.

The reverberations from Cibecue ran deep. Following Maj. Gen. Orlando Willcox's transfer from his post, Gen. George Crook once again became Arizona's military commander.

The additional troops sent to the territory might have frightened Juh, Geronimo, and other Chiricahua leaders living near San Carlos, according to historian Sidney Brinckerhoff.

On September 30, 1881, they broke out and headed for Mexico, killing 13 whites en route. "So as the White Mountain uprising of 1881 drew to a close, a new war, this with Geronimo, was begun," wrote Brinckerhoff.

As for the reasons behind the mutiny, they weren't hard to find. Perhaps the most compelling was that 13 of the scouts were from Cibecue, meaning they were being sent to arrest their own chief and medicine man.

"I also think the Indians were shocked that a force would come to their village and whisk away this important member of the tribe," said Collins, adding that the uprising feared by the military was highly unlikely.

But with the fear on both sides, many wild rumors, and almost no communication between Nock-ay-det-klinne and Carr, the climate for an explosion was ripe.

"Nothing like it happened again," said Collins. "But the military never entirely trusted its Indian scouts after Cibecue."

Sgt. Frank Mandeville, 6th Cavalry, wrote a poem reflecting the soldiers' view:

> *One by one we laid the corpse in,*
> *Earth to earth, ashes to ashes,*
> *Taps true. 'Tis still as death.*
> *Comrades murdered in the blue,*
> *By traitorous scouts at Cibicu.*

But bitterness lingered for both sides. Three weeks after the fight, when Carr returned to Cibecue hunting renegades, he found the bodies of his men had been dug up and mangled. Mutilation of dead enemies was relatively common among Apaches, but unearthing graves to get to them was highly unusual, perhaps another sign of rage at Nock-ay-det-klinne's death.

Carr described his grim find in a report to the Adjutant General: "Capt. Hentig's skull broken, brains gone, both feet and one hand cut off, and shot fired into his arms. Miller; head cut off and body dragged about but ring left on his finger, which will be sent to his sister. Livingstone and other's heads mashed and etc. Our war correspondent, Mr. Finerty, could not stand the stench."

The Prophet's body, either the whole of it or parts, was never recovered. He had told his disciples that if killed, and his body was cut to pieces, these would come together and he would be alive again in four days.

Some Apaches undoubtedly believed he had done just that.

CHAPTER EIGHT

Into the Sierra Madre

*General Crook needed a raid to justify an Army
incursion into Mexico — and the one he got
was the most stunning and violent of the war.*

———⋙•⋘———

W HEN GEN. GEORGE CROOK RETURNED IN SEPTEMBER 1882
to take command of the Army in Arizona, he immediately began planning one of the most dangerous
and difficult military operations of his career — penetration of
the Mexican Sierra Madre, the stronghold of the Chiricahua
Apaches who had jumped the reservation.

The mission had every reason to fail. But it did not, and
much of the credit goes to one man, a Cibecue Apache scout
who answered to the sweet-sounding nickname of Peaches. His
Apache names were Tzoe or Tso-ee, and Pa-na-yo-tishn, which
translates to "Coyote Saw Him."

His defection to the soldiers in April 1883, and his willingness to guide Crook to the renegade stronghold in Mexico,
was probably the most significant of the war.

The story of how this handsome, light-skinned 23-year-old
came to the general's side is one of drama, personal loss and
great good luck. But most of all it showed how the desires of a
single disaffected warrior could upset the balance of war.

Upon his return, Crook found the territory in a holy mess.
The big reservation at San Carlos had become a tinderbox.
Crook had long believed that mixing different tribes and bands
on the hot, dry flats east of Globe was a prescription for trouble, and his fear proved true.

Breakouts had become common, especially among the
Chiricahuas, and by 1882 some 200 of them were holed up in the

rugged Sierra Madre. As for the Indians who remained at San Carlos, they lived a miserable existence under Agent Joseph Tiffany, whose corrupt rule bred suspicion, distrust, and dangerous discontent.

"The constantly recurring outbreaks among the Indians and their consequent devastations were due to the criminal neglect or apathy of the Indian agent at San Carlos," reported a federal grand jury in Tucson.

But, as Crook declared, almost every Indian agent in the territory had done the same. They routinely stole supplies and food, forcing some Indians to near starvation. They also spread lies that the government, plotting to take Indian land, was going to disarm them and send them away to Oklahoma.

Under the circumstances, Crook told the Secretary of the Interior, the Apaches "had displayed remarkable forbearance in remaining at peace."

After restoring honest control at San Carlos, Crook turned his attention to the exiled Chiricahuas, a much thornier problem. He wanted desperately to bring them a fight. But under the terms of an agreement between the United States and Mexico, Crook was barred from going after the renegades, except under conditions of hot pursuit. That meant he needed a raid to justify an incursion — and the one he got was the most stunning and violent of the war.

At dusk on March 21, a 26-man war party, most likely led by Chatto, swept over the Huachuca Mountains and struck Clark's coal camp in the Canelo Hills, 12 miles from Fort Huachuca. The Apaches killed three workers on the outskirts of the camp. The men in the camp thought nothing of the shooting, figuring their fellow workers were hunting turkeys. They learned otherwise, according to the *Arizona Daily Star*, when a fourth victim, William Armstrong, suddenly took a bullet through his body, exclaiming, "I am killed! Look out, boys!"

Two others ran for cover in a tent, while P.R. Childs, who had the only gun in camp, ran down the creek and past the

ORIGINALLY FROM CIBECUE, TZOE BECAME AN ARMY SCOUT AFTER RECEIVING POOR TREATMENT AMONG THE CHIRICAHUAS.

Apaches. When he realized that the darkness prevented him from getting a good shot at them, Childs returned up the creek and hid in a small dugout near the tent. The Indians stopped behind a corral, 30 feet from the tent, and called in English and Spanish for the two men to come out.

When they didn't, the Indians fired into the tent, after which two of them — Tzoe and Be-ne-ac-ti-ney, which means "The Crazy Man" — ran toward it.

Childs shot and killed Be-ne-ac-ti-ney from the dugout. The Apaches returned fire, sending one bullet through Childs's hatband and shattering his rifle stock with another. Then, unsure how many more white men there were, the raiders ran off.

But Chatto's war party had only begun to kill. Over eight horrific days, they rampaged through southeastern Arizona and into New Mexico, killing 26 people. They moved so swiftly, covering as much as 100 miles in one day, that writer Eve Ball said the "military thought they were dealing with two or more war parties."

Among the dead was 52-year-old H.C. McComas, a federal judge, and his wife, Juniata. They were set upon while traveling in a buckboard between Silver City and Lordsburg, New Mexico. The judge was shot in four places, and his wife was hit by a bullet through the head. Both victims were found face down, stripped naked. Their possessions, including Juniata's bracelets and a diamond ring, had been stolen.

The killings of such a prominent couple outraged the nation. But even more emotionally riveting was the fate of the couple's six-year-old son, Charley, taken prisoner by the raiders. His story would become a national soap opera.

E ight months of calm preceding the rampage had lulled the territory into believing that Apache depredations had ended. When it became clear they hadn't, the reaction was that much more intense. Newspapers showed no mercy in ridiculing the military for not protecting the people. With sneering contempt, the *Tombstone Epitaph* noted that a group of that town's citizens was organizing to protect the soldiers.

"The hardy fellows who spend their days in the laborious task of sucking sutler whisky shall not be put in jeopardy," the paper wrote.

Hitting the same vigilante theme, the *Phoenix Herald* asked, "Is there no corporation, or man with lots of money, no county that will furnish funds to send a force after these fiends that will annihilate them?"

Crook, too, in a March 26 letter to the Secretary of the Interior, said he would "be glad to learn that the last of the Chiricahuas was under ground." He added, "It is believed they

CHIEF CHATTO, RESPONSIBLE FOR NUMEROUS RAIDS
AGAINST SETTLERS, LATER BECAME AN APACHE SCOUT.

have killed [in the last 10 years] not less than 1,000 persons in this country and in Mexico; they are constantly trying to stir up mischief among the Agency Indians, and so long as they can run back and forth across the border, this territory and New Mexico must look out for trouble. They are the worst band of Indians in America."

But the war party's rampage was significant for another reason. Be-ne-ac-ti-ney, the only casualty among Chatto's warriors at Clark's coal camp, was Tzoe's good friend, and his death evidently took the fight out of Tzoe. The Cibecue Apache deserted the war party a few days later.

Jason Betzinez, author of *I Fought With Geronimo*, and a cousin to Be-ne-ac-ti-ney, told of Tzoe's tearful departure as he stood atop a mountain looking toward his homeland.

"'Friends, you know I have been with you all through this hard and dangerous raid,' he said. "I have suffered when you have suffered. I have been hungry when you were without food. Now I have lost my best friend. I cannot go on. I'm going to leave you and return to my old home country.'"

In Betzinez's account, the other Indians gave Tzoe a friendly sendoff. But Tzoe told Crook something entirely different after he was arrested near San Carlos the morning of April 1.

In his book, *The Truth About Geronimo*, Britton Davis, San Carlos' temporary commander, wrote that he was in bed the night of March 31 when his door creaked open, and he saw an Indian standing over him, gun in hand.

"My revolver was on the bed beside me and I covered him with it as I asked who he was," Davis wrote. The Indian, one of Davis' spies, said in an excited whisper, "Chiricahua come."

The lieutenant, who had been anticipating a Chiricahua attack on San Carlos, bounded out of bed and rode 12 miles to a White Mountain Apache camp, accompanied by 30 of his scouts. There he found only Tzoe, who said he came in to get news of his mother and others of his family.

"He seemed little disturbed by his capture," Davis wrote, "and smiled faintly when I took his knife and cartridge belt off of him. My scouts had his rifle."

The prisoner was taken to see Crook in Willcox. Through interpreters, the two engaged in a lengthy discussion, the particulars of which were recorded in a diary written by Crook's aide, John Bourke.

Contrary to Betzinez's story, Tzoe said he escaped from the war party in the hills near Railroad Pass east of Willcox. "I saw my chance, took off my moccasins and crept out into the rocks and walked about on them so they couldn't find any trail," Tzoe said.

"When morning came, they hunted for me without success."

He also portrayed his affiliation with the Chiricahuas as vaguely hostile, beginning with a raid on San Carlos, in April of 1882, by Geronimo, Chatto, Naiche and Chihuahua. These renegades rode across the border and herded other Chiricahuas off the reservation and down into Mexico.

Tzoe was among those taken. Although he was a Cibecue Apache, he later explained that two of his wives and his small child were Chiricahuas, and he was forced to leave San Carlos along with them.

Shortly after this outbreak, Tzoe's two wives and his child were killed in a fight in Mexico, and Tzoe himself badly wounded.

He remained with the Chiricahuas through the winter, even though, he claimed, they watched him suspiciously and forced him to cook and do other chores for them.

"When they started on this raid, I was very glad," he said. "I knew each day would bring me nearer to my relatives on the San Carlos, and I hoped to be able to get away from the Chiricahuas and run back to the agency."

Whether that is entirely true is difficult now to say. He was known to be close friends with Chatto, and when he and Benac-ti-ney charged the two white men in the Canelo Hills, he certainly wasn't behaving as a reluctant warrior.

As for the McComas killings, Tzoe never mentioned them in his interview, and based on the timetable in his narrative, he departed the band before the couple was butchered. Had he confessed to being part of the band at the time of the high-profile McComas killings, he would have faced the possibility of execution.

But he probably told the truth. As Bourke once said of Tzoe, "His absolute veracity and fidelity in all his dealings [was] a notable feature in his character."

Crook listened intently as the defector talked over a range of subjects.

The purpose of Chatto's raid was to acquire ammunition, although the warriors also intended, as Tzoe said, "to kill every-

NAICHE, YOUNGEST SON OF COCHISE, POSES WITH GERONIMO.

one they met. It didn't make any difference whether they had guns or not."

This brutality stemmed from the treatment the Chiricahuas had received from Tiffany.

"It was on account of that agent with the big stomach," Tzoe said. "He used to kick them with his fists and cuff and beat them and all his employees got to doing the same. He treated them badly in every way. . . . He threatened to have them removed from San Carlos to a far-distant country, so the Chiricahuas broke out and went on the warpath."

Tzoe also described the Sierra Madre stronghold of the Chiricahuas and said the condition of the renegades was grim.

Food was scarce and many of them hoped to return to San Carlos. But the "country down there is full of Mexican troops," and, he complained, the border area was full of American troops and their scouts.

Only 70 fighting men remained, Tzoe said. They were well-supplied with 16-shot rifles, but little ammunition. The renegades also included "fifty well grown boys" and a large number of women and children.

When Tzoe offered to guide the soldiers into the Sierra Madre, Crook accepted, believing that in the discontent of this striking-looking Apache he had found a way to defeat an implacable enemy. Soon the tireless defector who never was out of humor came to be known among the troops as Peaches, for his soft, peach-like complexion.

With characteristic deliberation, the general organized his expedition, including getting Mexican consent to cross the border. Foremost in his mind was recovering Charley McComas, the little boy whose name had come to symbolize to the nation the very depths of the Apache menace.

Crook's command left San Bernardino Springs, in southeastern Arizona, on May 1. With him were 42 enlisted men of the 6th Cavalry; 11 officers; a collection of interpreters, mule packers and chiefs of scouts; and 193 Indian scouts wearing red headbands to distinguish them from the renegades.

The mission was eerie in its first days, crossing a once-populated land that lay burnt and empty due to Chiricahua raiding. Soon the terrain became so rough that every man, including Crook, had to dismount and walk, according to a diary kept by an unnamed soldier, published on the front page of the *Arizona Daily Star*.

On the night of May 8, as the men made their way deep into the Sierra Madre, they camped on a mountain plateau, 7000 feet high. "The country is grand and gloomy," the diarist wrote, "the whole face of nature being cut by immense gorges and mountains apparently piled one on top of the other."

The next day, five pack mules lost their footing on a torturous trail and plunged into a deep chasm below. "The country is almost impassable," marveled the diarist, "and looks as if passage of man had been barred by the hand of the Almighty."

In the village of Huachinera, Tzoe told the soldiers that when he had passed through there with Chatto and his raiders in March, 16 of the warriors walked boldly into the town plaza in daylight and bought tobacco from a frightened vendor.

On May 11, the diarist wrote: "Captain Crawford, Lieutenants Gatewood and McKey took 150 scouts and provisions for a foot scout of three days, Tzoe having informed General Crook that the command was nearing the stronghold . . ."

Three days later, Crawford found fresh Indian signs, evidence of a camp ahead. It turned out to be Chatto's. On May 15, as his scouts moved into position to attack, they stumbled upon some Chiricahuas and opened fire before Crawford was ready.

Various stories have been told about how the fight began, including one involving a scout bumping into renegades as he broke from the group to relieve himself.

However it happened, the premature start might have doomed Charley McComas. Author Betzinez said that after an old woman was killed in the initial firing on the camp, her son, an Apache nicknamed Speedy, became so enraged that he beat McComas to death with rocks.

To protect one of their band from possible punishment, Betzinez wrote that the Apaches later lied to the soldiers, saying "the little boy had run off into the brush and was never found."

The beating story came from eyewitness Ramona Chihuahua, daughter of Chief Chihuahua. By publishing it in his 1959 book, Betzinez solved a morbid mystery that has produced a number of bizarre theories on the child's fate.

One writer even tells of a Norwegian explorer in Mexico, who, in 1938, thought he had found proof that the boy had wandered with fugitive Apaches for 50 years until mysteriously slain. The explorer's evidence? He found traces of hair in an Apache comb that might have come from McComas's head.

Crawford's scouts killed four men and six women, captured 28 ponies and a sizeable cache of supplies. As battles go, it was minor.

B ut Crook's thrust into the Chiricahua lair was a devastating psychological blow. One of those captured, the daughter of the chief Bonito, said her people had been thoroughly dismayed to see Apache scouts wearing red headbands charging toward them with Tzoe, who had recently been among them, in the lead. Now they knew that no place was safe.

Using a captured Apache woman as a courier, Crook sent the renegades a message: "Surrender within three days or I will kill all of you."

Over the next days, demoralized and exhausted Apaches came in to Crook's camp, slowly at first, then in numbers. Tzoe himself went into the mountains alone to convince many of them, including Geronimo, to give up.

By May 28, some 374 Chiricahuas — 123 men and 251 women and children — had surrendered, along with the chiefs Nana, Loco, and Bonito.

Crook agreed to allow other chiefs to report to San Carlos later, after they had collected their scattered women and children. When Geronimo, the last of them, arrived on the reservation in April 1884, it appeared, as Crook's biographer Martin Schmitt noted, the general had "performed the incredible feat of subduing the Chiricahuas eight months after taking command of the department."

Although that wasn't the case, the Sierra Madre operation was exactly what Bourke called it — "one of the boldest and most successful strokes ever achieved by an officer of the United States Army."

However, it couldn't have been accomplished without Tzoe, the scout that soldiers called Peaches. But to the Chiricahuas he was a hated man, known thereafter as Yellow Wolf in contempt for his treachery.

A Killing That Shocked the Nation

Eastern newspapers, including
The New York Times, *devoted front-page space*
to the issue, some demanding retribution for
what they believed was murder. Even Gen. George
Crook called the killing an assassination.

———◆———

T HE KILLING OF CAPT. EMMET CRAWFORD, 3RD CAVALRY,
made news around America, and it should have. His
death in the Mexican Sierra Madre, on January 11,
1886, lengthened by nine months the final roundup of the renegade Chiricahuas, and probably cost a hundred additional lives,
as well as untold losses of stock and other property. It also
played a role in the second dismissal of Gen. George Crook as
Arizona's military commander.

But what drew the most attention was the villainy of
Crawford's killers, and their identity. He wasn't shot down by
renegade Apaches in the midst of a firefight, but by a supposed
ally, a rifleman in a company of Mexican militia formed to kill
Chiricahuas and stop their depredations.

At the time the fatal round was fired, the captain was
standing, in uniform, atop a rock and waving a white handkerchief. To add a surreal touch to an already strange story,
the wily Geronimo saw the encounter from a nearby hilltop,
and as he watched, he dissolved in laughter.

The clock began ticking for Crawford with another of
Geronimo's outbreaks, this one from Turkey Creek on May 17,
1885. The warrior was accompanied by chiefs Naiche, Mangas,

OLD NANA, ONE OF THE LAST
OF THE WARRING APACHE CHIEFS.

Chihuahua, and Nana and 144 Chiricahuas. Knowing that another expedition into Mexico would be necessary, Crook ordered the formation of an all-Indian force to pursue the renegades.

Crawford, who had organized and commanded the scouts at San Carlos, had said he wanted no regular army troops with him on future operations in the Sierra Madre. In terms of strength, cunning, and almost unlimited endurance, Crawford had learned, no white soldier could match Arizona's mountain Indians in that brutal terrain.

The stature of the Philadelphia-born officer — a veteran of the Civil War, campaigns against the Sioux, and Crook's 1883 Sierra Madre expedition — lent his voice considerable authority.

Lt. Britton Davis, in his book *The Truth About Geronimo*, described Crawford as a modest, self-effacing and kindly man who delighted in assigning credit to his subordinates.

"Crawford was born a thousand years too late," Davis wrote. "Mentally, morally and physically he would have been an ideal knight of King Arthur's Court. Six feet one, gray-eyed, untiring, he was an ideal cavalryman."

His influence extended to the Indians under his command. He had earned their trust by speaking up on their behalf, occasionally at risk to his own standing, and none of them questioned his bravery.

The captain's handling of Dutchy was an example of his methods, according to Lt. William E. Shipp.

In the summer of 1884, Dutchy had mutinied and was sent to Fort Bowie in irons. Shipp, writing in the December 1892 edition of the *Journal of the U.S. Cavalry Association*, noted that although Dutchy's guilt was not in doubt, Crawford took him back as a scout, but refused to give him the chevrons he demanded.

"He [Crawford] selected him as his body servant, and trusted implicitly this man who had not long before threatened his life," Shipp wrote. "The result was the establishment of a complete ascendancy over Dutchy, and increased respect on the part of the others, as they saw how little he feared this dangerous man."

Crawford's all-Indian scout battalion, consisting of 100 Chiricahua and White Mountain Apaches, crossed the border into Sonora, Mexico, on December 11, 1885. Another all-Indian command, led by Capt. Wirt Davis, crossed into Chihuahua about the same time.

Crawford's men saw no trace of the renegades for three weeks. The terrain was so rough the troops hobbled their horses at a base camp near Nacori, on the west slope of the Sierra Madre, and proceeded on foot. Then, early in January, the scouts found their first Indian sign and concluded that Geronimo and Naiche were camped at a place named Devil's Backbone.

To maintain surprise, every man in the troop — including Crawford, Lt. Marion Maus, interpreter Tom Horn, a doctor and a hospital steward, and Shipp — wore moccasins to avoid making noise. They were thin-soled, Shipp wrote, which "allowed

**EMMET CRAWFORD'S AIDE, DUTCHY,
AVENGED THE CAPTAIN'S DEATH.**

the feet to feel every stone of the million that lay in the path."

The men were limited to one blanket each, and the nights were bitterly cold. The scouts built small, smokeless fires from dry wood in daytime. At night, the fires were hidden from view in a gully or depression. In crossing ridges, the men were careful never to expose their bodies against the skyline.

By January 9, the command had located the renegade camp, about 40 miles southeast of Nacori. Crawford went there with his men on a grueling, 12-mile night march over steep mountains and stiletto underbrush that left their clothing literally in tatters.

At dawn on January 10, after 48 hours without sleep, Crawford moved his men into position for a surprise attack. His surprise was lost when some donkeys in the Indian camp sensed the presence of the approaching force and began braying. Crawford's scouts fired on the renegades who were gathering the donkeys. The renegades quickly scattered, leaving behind their entire camp outfit and all their horses. Only one

PHOTOGRAPHER C.S. FLY CAPTURED
GERONIMO'S MAKESHIFT CAMP IN THE SIERRA MADRE
PRIOR TO THE APACHE LEADER'S SURRENDER.

renegade was wounded because, Shipp said, the soliders had difficulty distinguishing the renegades from their own force.

"It was impossible for us to tell friends from foes," he wrote. "Every time I myself attempted to shoot I was stopped, because I was about to shoot a scout. At last, in desperation, I fired two shots at some figure dimly seen. Who he was I never knew, for I missed him."

Later that day, an elderly woman approached and told Crawford that Geronimo and Naiche were ready to surrender and would come in to meet him the next morning.

"The hostiles were without any food or camp outfit, and had no animals," wrote Lieutenant Maus, in a letter to Crook 11 days later. "Had this talk taken place, I believe most of the band would have surrendered."

That night, the exhausted command slept well. But Crawford, believing all danger had passed, did not post sentries. The otherwise brilliant captain could not have anticipated the conspiracy of events about to occur.

At dawn, the camp was roused from sleep by shouting

and gunfire. No one was certain what was happening or why, and the confusion was compounded by a heavy fog over the mountains.

A Mexican militia group, numbering about 150 men, was nearing Crawford's camp when they heard Apache voices and began shooting.

Crawford, Maus, and Horn ran toward the action, thinking it was Captain Davis' scouts firing at them by mistake. When the three Americans realized the shooters were Mexican, they waved handkerchiefs and shouted, "*Soldados Americanos! Soldados Americanos!*" Even at that, the firing continued for 15 minutes.

"It then seemed that we had made them understand that we were American soldiers," wrote Maus in his letter to Crook. "They answered they would not fire, but all the time moved toward a hill a short distance away, a little higher than our position."

Several of the Mexicans stepped forward to talk. But Crawford's scouts, still keyed up, escalated the tension by rattling the breechlocks on their rifles. The captain quickly ordered Maus to make sure none of his men fired. Maus had just started back to do so when the Mexicans opened another volley.

"When I turned again," wrote Maus, "I saw the captain lying on the rocks with a wound in his head and some of his brains upon the rocks. . . . It is remarkable no others were shot. There can be no mistake: these men knew they were firing at American soldiers."

Shipp gave this account in *The Cavalry Association Journal*:

"He [Crawford] now appeared on a high rock conspicuous above every other object. It is impossible to tell how he viewed the situation, though he must have known that in so exposing himself he ran a great risk, no matter under what circumstances the attack had been made.

"Thinking, no doubt, that by exposing himself to full view in his uniform, he might save us from being again attacked, he did not hesitate, but climbed the rock and stood waving a white handkerchief in token of peace. In a moment a single shot rang out, followed by a volley. Crawford fell . . ."

At the same instant, Shipp wrote, Dutchy, the once-mutinous Indian to whom Crawford had entrusted his life, rose up from his perch 28 paces away and shot the captain's assassin. Also at the same time, one of the militiamen leveled his rifle at Horn, who was shouting angrily in Spanish, and shot the guide through the arm.

A second gunfight erupted. It lasted 30 minutes and featured a spectator's gallery that included Geronimo himself, according to Angie Debo, his biographer.

As the firing tapered off, Maus and Horn again went to meet the Mexicans. One of the company's officers said they thought they were shooting at hostile Apaches and, according to Maus, "seemed sincere in their regrets."

"They asked me for horses to take their wounded away and wanted rations," wrote Maus, who had now assumed command. "I promised to do what I could."

In addition to Horn's flesh wound, two of Crawford's scouts were slightly wounded, and another was shot through both legs. The Mexicans suffered about five wounded and four killed, including the militia's commander, Mauricio Corredor. Corredor had shot and killed the Apache chief Victorio in October 1880, earning a 2,000-peso bounty from the Mexican government and a nickel-plated rifle.

The next day, January 12, Maus and Shipp learned the Mexicans' true motives in firing on their command. As Maus was building litters for his wounded and readying his command for the march home, he was summoned to the Mexican camp on the pretext of discussing the horses he had loaned them. As soon he entered the camp, Maus was surrounded by hard-looking men, not in any uniform but dressed in ordinary cotton clothes, wearing moccasins or rawhide sandals, and carrying .44-caliber Remington rifles. One of Maus's interpreters, named Concepcion, had already been taken captive.

The Mexicans behaved in a threatening manner and asked to see his papers, which had been left with the pack train. They also told Maus he had no authority in Mexico, in spite of a treaty allowing either country's soldiers to pursue renegades across the border.

"They asked me for six mules to take their wounded," Maus wrote. "I did not expect to get away. But I told them that on word of my honor, I would send them if they would let me go back. They refused to take the ponies, as they said they were worthless."

Crawford's scouts, aware that Maus had been taken prisoner, shouted angrily at the Mexicans and appeared ready to fight to get him back. Only then was Maus permitted to go.

Based on this episode, Maus and Shipp concluded that the Mexicans' true intent was to drive Crawford and his men back, then steal their stock and camp supplies.

"That plunder was their intent in attacking us is certain," wrote Shipp. "They saw only a few white men, and the fire of the scouts was so weak at first that they had no reason to believe us a large party."

Later that day, Geronimo and Naiche came to the American camp and told Maus they wanted to talk, but only to Crook. On January 13, nine of the renegades surrendered, including Chief Nana, the wife and children of both Geronimo and Naiche, and Geronimo's sister.

"Of course the chiefs will meet with you, if you wish, near the line," wrote Maus to Crook. "There they will have a talk and, I think, surrender to you. They are tired of being out. I think they wish to meet you in a month. Meanwhile they do not intend to do any acts of hostility. I believe these people mean to do as they say. . . . They have scarcely anything and are poor and miserable."

Maus started his command on the difficult journey home. Shipp described the men carrying the wounded on litters made of canvas stretched between bundles of cane. The cane was so pliable and clumsy it took eight scouts to carry each one. The moccasins the men wore were torn to pieces on the wet ground, forcing them to walk barefoot over the stones.

Maus said the gloom cast over the command by the death of Crawford, "to whom we were all much attached, and who has so faithfully done all possible to accomplish the object for which we were sent, has been very depressing."

At Nacori, Maus buried Crawford under a pile of rocks, his body wrapped only in a blanket. The captain died January 18, seven days and four hours after taking a .50-caliber bullet to the head. Crook later ordered a party back into Mexico to retrieve the body for a proper burial in a family plot in Kearney, Nebraska.

Eight years later, Maus was awarded the Medal of Honor for his gallantry in the Sierra Madre.

Crawford's death shocked Americans. Eastern newspapers, including *The New York Times*, devoted front-page space to the issue, some demanding retribution for what they believed was murder.

Even Crook, in his report to the Secretary of War, called the killing an assassination, noting that the fatal round "seemed to be an agreed-upon signal, as at once the firing became general."

For several months, officials of both governments lobbed accusations back and forth. But nothing came of it. The Mexicans refused to pay reparations or take any responsibility, even charging Maus with lying and suggesting that Crawford's own scouts killed him.

Had the captain not died, the Apache Wars might have ended the next day. Crook himself said that Crawford was thoroughly known to all the Indians and had their confidence and that Geronimo and Naiche probably would have surrendered on the spot.

As it was, the war dragged on for nine more months, costing more lives and destruction, and forcing citizens of two countries to live in abject fear.

The episode — particularly the half-hearted scout attack on Geronimo's camp — also deepened the doubts of the Army's commanding general, Philip H. Sheridan, about the willingness of the Chiricahua scouts to fire on their own people. His increasing lack of faith in their work, versus Crook's unwavering support, was a factor in Crook's leaving his Arizona command three months later.

Perhaps more than anything else, however, Crawford's death demonstrated how the ambitions of great nations, and the lives of the men charged with fulfilling them, can turn on the slightest twist of fate.

What if that ragtag Mexican militia had not found its way to Crawford's camp on a foggy January morning?

"It was a strange mischance that caused these two commands to meet at this particular time, and in a country perhaps never before traversed by similar parties," wrote Lieutenant Shipp, who was killed in action at San Juan, Cuba, in July 1898. "Different as they were, either might have done good work but for the presence of the other."

CHAPTER TEN

A Sincere Surrender Scuttled

"Once I moved about like the wind.
Now I surrender to you and that is all."
— Geronimo

———◆———

L ATE IN MARCH 1886, 10 WEEKS AFTER CAPT. EMMET Crawford was killed [see story in Chapter Nine], Lt. Marion Maus notified Gen. George Crook that the renegade Chiricahuas were ready to surrender. Again it looked as if this bitter and protracted war would end. Once more, however, Crook's long-sought peace was aborted — this time through double-dealing on Geronimo's part, with help from a mysterious Swiss-born rancher.

Charles F. Tribolet walked onto the stage of history for a brief time, meddled in affairs to the detriment of all, then departed without leaving clear footprints. A bootlegger and frequent buyer of stolen cattle whose strict interest was money, Tribolet made pocketfuls selling liquor to the Indians, and Geronimo was a good customer.

The combination was explosive. It led directly to Crook's decision, on April 2, 1886, to step aside as commander of the Department of Arizona.

In a war marked by strange friendships and complicated loyalties, it's worth noting that Crook's resignation was accepted by his old West Point classmate, Lt. Gen. Philip Sheridan, commanding general of the Army.

For a time, Crook appeared to be accomplishing his mission. In response to Maus's message, the general left Fort Bowie on the morning of March 22, accompanied by Capt. John

THIS DETAIL OF A GROUP SHOT SHOWS PACKERS AND INTERPRETERS WHO ACCOMPANIED GENERAL CROOK'S STAFF.

Gregory Bourke and others. Riding alongside the general's ambulance were White Mountain Apaches, Alchesay and Kayetenna, whom Crook hoped would act as emissaries.

They made the 90-mile trip to John Slaughter's San Bernardino Ranch, outside Douglas, without an escort, and from there rode on horseback to Maus's camp 25 miles into Sonora, Mexico, in Canyon de los Embudos.

As they approached, Kayetenna rode off to hunt some wild pigs. When Crook and his aide, Capt. Cyrus Roberts, heard shooting, they rode toward the sound and ran right into Geronimo, Naiche, and several other Apaches. The men whose surrender Crook sought then guided Crook's party toward Maus's camp.

The Indian encampment was only 500 yards distant, perched atop a rocky hill, surrounded by ravines and canyons through which they could escape to higher peaks if attacked.

**GENERAL CROOK, WEARING HIS TRADEMARK
PITH HELMET, AND GERONIMO, SEATED LEFT OF CENTER,
NEGOTIATE SURRENDER TERMS.**

In his official report, Crook said the Apaches were in superb physical condition, armed to the teeth with all the ammunition they could carry, and "fierce as so many tigers." He wrote, "In manner they were suspicious, and at the same time confident and self-reliant."

By agreeing to meet without regular Army troops to defend him, the general knew he was placing his life on the line. However, he had no choice. Geronimo had dictated the terms to Maus, insisting that no troops be present and naming the place and time, the latter conveyed by smoke signals. Crook wanted to meet on U.S. soil, but no argument would move the Apaches.

"Into their hands I must trust myself," he wrote, "or back they would go to their mountain fastness."

After Crook ate his lunch that day, the first conference between the two sides began. The Chiricahua leaders sat on the stream bank while some 24 warriors, armed with Winchester repeating rifles and Springfield breech-loading Army rifles, sat nearby.

In addition to Crook, the Army contingent consisted of four officers — Roberts, Maus, and Lieutenants William Shipp and S.L. Faison. Charles Strauss, the ex-mayor of Tombstone, was there, as were several interpreters and mule packers.

Also present were Captain Roberts's 11-year-old son, Charlie, and 14-year-old Jimmy Howell, the little brother of John Slaughter's wife, Viola. Evidently afraid of missing a great adventure, Jimmy caught up with the general's ambulance as it rolled south and was allowed to stay.

Bourke, in his book *On The Border With Crook*, described the setting: "The whole ravine was romantically beautiful: shading the rippling water were smooth, white-trunked, long, and slender sycamores, dark gnarly ash, rough-barked cottonwoods, pliant willows, briary buckthorn."

The strangeness of the event was compounded by the presence of Tombstone's persistent photographer, C.S. Fly and his assistant. In spite of the great tension, Bourke said that Fly still "saw his opportunity, and improved it fully" by taking snapshots of Geronimo and the others.

"With a nerve that would have reflected undying glory on a Chicago drummer, Fly coolly asked Geronimo and the warriors with him to change positions, and turn their heads or faces, to improve the negative. None of them seemed to mind him in the least except Chihuahua, who kept dodging behind a tree."

The next day, Fly ventured boldly into the Indian camp to take more pictures. His work constitutes the only known photographs of a wartime Indian camp, although Bourke thought Fly was "a damned fool" who might "never come out."

The meeting did not go well. Geronimo went into a long-winded explanation of his breakout from Turkey Creek the year before and insisted that the return of the Chiricahuas to the reservation be accompanied by a grant of amnesty.

Crook, wearing simple canvas pants and a duck coat, was in no mood for bargaining. The two argued in the frankest terms, with Crook demanding from Geronimo what he had been

**CHIRICAHUA WARRIORS FLANK
THE LEADER OF THEIR BAND, GERONIMO.**

authorized by Washington to get — unconditional surrender followed by exile to the East. Several times Crook sarcastically corrected the renegade's claims about past events and assured him he would hear no more, finally drawing the line.

"There is no use for you to try to talk nonsense," Crook said. "I am no child. You must make up your minds whether to stay on the warpath or surrender unconditionally. If you stay out I'll keep after you and kill the last one if it takes fifty years. . . . I have said all I have to say. You had better think it over tonight and let me know in the morning."

Geronimo appeared shocked at such frankness. Sweat dripped from his temples and his hands, and he clutched nervously at a buckskin thong.

The conference ended with an agreement to meet again in two days. Crook wired Sheridan, informing him that it had not gone well, and dispatched Kayetenna as a spy to the Indian camp. He found the Apaches in a highly agitated state, as likely to open fire as surrender.

But on the morning of March 27, Crook received word that Chief Chihuahua was coming in with his band, and when he did, Geronimo and Naiche came with him. The conference resumed, with each of the leaders speaking directly to Crook.

In order to win the surrender of all three leaders, Crook

had to soften his terms. The Chiricahuas asked that their families be allowed to accompany them in their deportation from Fort Bowie and that they be returned to the reservation within two years.

Knowing he had to act immediately, Crook dropped his demand for unconditional surrender and accepted those terms. Washington had told him to make no promises to the Apaches unless it was absolutely necessary to obtain their surrender — and Crook clearly believed it was necessary.

Transcripts of the chiefs' remarks were reprinted in Lt. Britton Davis' book, *The Truth About Geronimo*. In abridged form, here is what they said:

"It seems to me I have seen the one who makes the rain and sends the winds," Chihuahua said. "He must have sent you to this place. I surrender simply to you because I believe in you, and you have never lied to us."

Naiche was next: "What Chihuahua said, I say. I surrender to you just the same as he did. I give you my word; I give you my body. I surrender. I have nothing more to say than that."

Then Geronimo added his words, interrupting his talk at several points to shake Crook's hand:

"Two or three words are enough. I have but little to say. I surrender myself to you. We are comrades, all one family, all one band. What the others say, I say also. I give myself up to you. Do with me what you please. I surrender. Once I moved about like the wind. Now I surrender to you and that is all. . . .

"I have no lies in my heart. Whatever you tell me is true. We are all satisfied of that. I hope the day may come when my word shall be as strong with you as yours is with me. That is all I have to say."

But surrender did not relax the Chiricahuas' vigilance. Crook said they kept mounted and constantly on watch, with no more than eight of them remaining in the Army camp at one time.

On the morning of March 28, 1886, the general hastily departed for Fort Bowie, eager to have telegraphic communication with the War Department. Maus and his 80 Chiricahua scouts, the same battalion that had fought the Mexican militia in the Sierra Madre, were charged with escorting the prisoners to Bowie.

The first day, Maus' command camped at an Army supply camp 12 miles south of San Bernardino, and the second day at Smuggler's Springs, just below the border.

The role in this drama of the rascal Tribolet, who ran a ranch a few hundred yards south of the border, didn't begin until the night of March 29. He had been selling whiskey and mescal to the Indians as well as to American officers before Crook arrived, and when the talks began, Maus expelled him from camp.

But he was persistent, refusing, as he had for some time, to stop. "There's no way of dealing with Tribolet," Crook once complained. "He has been tried before but bought his way out. . . . Why, that man has a beef contract for our Army."

Charles Lummis, a Los Angeles journalist, reported that Tribolet boasted of the amount of whiskey he had sold to the Apaches and that he had once given a bottle of champagne to Geronimo.

"Why," Tribolet said, referring to the Apaches, "it's money in my pocket to have those fellows out."

Even after being tossed out of Maus' camp, the bootlegger returned each night to sell to his wares. He did so, as usual, on March 29, only this time he added to his night's work by convincing some of the Indians they would be hung once they crossed the line. Frightened and drunk, and with a cold drizzle falling, Geronimo and Naiche bolted, taking with them 20 men, 13 women, three boys and three girls.

When news of the surrender reached Sheridan, he carried it to President Grover Cleveland, who found Crook's terms too liberal. Sheridan wired back on March 30:

"The President cannot assent to the surrender of the hos-

**C.S. FLY RECORDED THE APACHE SURRENDER
IN CANYON DE LOS EMBUDOS.**

tiles on the terms of their imprisonment East for two years. . . .
He instructs you to enter again into negotiations on the terms
of their unconditional surrender, only sparing their lives."

Sheridan added: "You are directed to take every precaution
against the escape of the hostiles, which must not be allowed
under any circumstances."

By then, the renegades were gone, which Sheridan learned the
same day. It set off a flurry of angry telegrams back and
forth. Sheridan criticized the Chiricahua scouts for not knowing of the breakout ahead of time.

Crook defended his scout battalion, insisting they were
thoroughly loyal. He tried to explain to Sheridan the almost
impossible character of the country in which his men operated
and the nature of the renegades.

"Persons not thoroughly conversant with both," he wrote,
dropping a thinly veiled insult, "can have no conception" of
these difficulties.

But it was all over for Crook. With his surrender terms
scuttled by Washington, he could no longer negotiate, and if he
had tried to do so on Cleveland's terms, the Indians would have
scattered to the mountains.

As it was, 77 Apaches stayed put. They arrived at Fort Bowie on April 2. Among them were Chihuahua, two of Geronimo's wives and three of his children, Naiche's family, and the relatives of all those warriors who had fled.

In his resignation telegram, Crook insisted his plan for ending the conflict was the one most likely to succeed, then added:

"It may be, however, that I am too much wedded to my own views in this matter, and as I have spent nearly eight years of the hardest work of my life in this department, I respectfully request that I may now be relieved of its command."

Word of Geronimo's latest double cross put the territory in an uproar. Its citizens, led by an outraged press, had been insisting for some time that Geronimo hang for his murders. Now the papers added Crook to their list of targets.

Actually, the calumny was nothing new to the general. Newspapers had been damning him repeatedly. Even with lies telegraphed from one end of the country to the other, Lummis said Crook never let out a word in his own defense.

"He feels it — no doubt — he would be more than man if the poisoned shafts did not sting," the journalist wrote. But he said Crook's goal was "to fight, not to justify himself."

And Lummis added this tribute: "I like the grim old general. There is that in him which makes one want to take off one's hat."

But Lummis wasn't entirely correct. Crook certainly was taciturn and ordinarily not prone to trumpeting his accomplishments. Yet he made an exception after the Embudos matter, in which he believed his honor had been stained.

After leaving Arizona, the general went to Nebraska to begin his new assignment in the Department of the Platte. Omaha's citizens, delighted to see him return, organized a banquet in his honor. Amid a roomful of supporters, Crook rose and said:

"The military critic in Washington, that parody on manhood, who probably never heard a hostile in his life, realizes the truth of the old adage that one campaign in Washington is worth a dozen in the field."

And a few weeks later, he told the *Army and Navy Journal* that nine-tenths of all the dispatches sent out by the Associated Press "in regard to my operations against the Apaches have not had one grain of truth in them."

Crook even compiled and published a 25-page brochure — titled "Resumé of Operations Against Apache Indians, 1882-1886" — defending his handling of the war. He always insisted that the Chiricahua surrender was sincere and that Geronimo and Naiche "stampeded" only after being "filled with fiery mescal, and alarmed by the lies of a designing man."

The matter must have worked on Crook's mind for years. On January 2, 1890, when he again met his old Apache adversaries, this time at the Mount Vernon Barracks in Alabama, Crook asked what happened that night in March 1886.

Naiche said he was afraid he would be taken somewhere he didn't like. "I thought that all who were taken away would die," he said. Geronimo feared the territory's citizens "were going to arrest and hang me."

As for Tribolet, the bootlegger who thwarted Crook's plans, he faded from view following the escape of the Chiricahuas, and what became of him remains unknown. It seems the perfect epitaph for a man described by a Tucson judge as "one of the worst scoundrels that ever went unhung."

CHAPTER ELEVEN

Wrangling for Glory

He arrived in full uniform on a fresh horse,
showing all the pomp and vanity of a general
who did not attend West Point and was
deeply conscious of it. In this and other episodes
of his career, Gen. Nelson Miles earned his
nickname, the "Brave Peacock."

———◆———

O
N APRIL 2, 1886, GEN. NELSON APPLETON MILES RECEIVED
orders to take command of the Department of Arizona.
Five months later, Geronimo and Naiche and their followers were in custody. The end should have been a time of
huzzahs for the victors. However, the celebration was marred
by a jealousy-driven feud between Miles and Gen. George Crook
that diminished their reputations.

The wrangling for glory, by them and others, smoldered
like a fire that blew into a blaze and scorched everything near
it, even consuming the reputation of Lt. Charles Gatewood, 6th
Cavalry, without whom Geronimo's surrender couldn't have
been accomplished.

The two generals had disliked each other for years as
they competed for the title of the country's foremost Indian
fighter. Crook seemed to have the advantage, especially after
his brilliant Winter Campaign of 1872-73 against the Apaches,
for which he received a double promotion from lieutenant
colonel to brigadier general.

Historian John A. Carroll, in the spring 1967 edition of
The Smoke Signal, published in Tucson, wrote that the promotion vaulted Crook over more qualified officers, including Miles,
who resented the snub. Despite far out-performing Crook in

**GEN. NELSON A. MILES, CROOK'S SUCCESSOR
AS COMMANDER OF THE DEPARTMENT OF ARIZONA.**

the Sioux campaign of 1876-77, Miles wouldn't make brigadier until 1880.

Miles began his Arizona assignment determined to outshine Crook, his predecessor. On April 11, 1886, Miles's ambulance pulled up outside Crook's office at Fort Bowie. Author Peter DeMontravel, Miles's most recent biographer, noted that the boom of 6-pound cannons greeted the general's arrival, but the pomp of the moment was diminished as the 46-year-old Miles, who had recently gained weight, struggled to fit through the door of the mule-drawn wagon.

Another reporter, however, described the new commander more flatteringly as a "tall, straight, fine-looking man of 210 pounds" with a "well-modeled head, high brow, strong eye, clean-cut aquiline nose and firm mouth. . . . an imposing soldierly figure all around."

USING NO APACHE SCOUTS, CAPT. HENRY LAWTON
PURSUED APACHE RENEGADES IN MEXICO
FOR FOUR MONTHS WITHOUT SUCCESS.

His heart heavy with failure, Crook shook hands with his successor. He must have been bitter. As recently as January, with Geronimo still eluding Crook, *The New York Times* reported that Miles had been jockeying behind the scenes to replace him.

The new commander's orders were to "carry on the most vigorous operations looking to the destruction or capture of the hostiles" — without the conditions Crook was allowed to offer — and to do so with the prominent use of regular troops. In other words, the scouts would play a minor role, a dictum that greatly offended Crook and the officers who had served with him.

Miles organized a force under Capt. Henry Lawton, 4th Cavalry, with Leonard Wood, a young Harvard-trained physician, assisting. He chose Lawton and Wood for their physical strength, courage and high-spiritedness, qualities the general believed would allow them to keep pace with the Apaches in a punishing campaign.

In this, Miles was delusional. The truth was as Crook knew it: Without some use of diplomacy to induce their surrender, no force of white men had the skill to penetrate the Mexican stronghold and either kill the renegades or bring them out.

"Those twenty men will last twenty years," said Crook

through a sympathetic newspaper reporter, his preferred method of spreading the anti-Miles viewpoint.

Lawton and Wood proved this by thrashing about along the border and in Mexico for four months following their May 5 departure from Fort Huachuca. They covered more than 3,000 miles, endured blazing temperatures, nearly deadly thirst, terrible weight loss, and "damnable gnats, flies and mosquitoes" that made it impossible to sleep.

Yet they failed to kill or capture a single Indian.

With 5,000 troops at his disposal, charged with ferreting out 20 men and 13 women, Miles recognized that he faced a humiliation as large as Crook's at Embudos. His solution was to return to Crook's tactics — using Chiricahua scouts and diplomacy backed by rifles.

On July 14, Miles quietly sent two Chiricahua scouts — Martine and Kayitah — along with Gatewood, into Mexico to find Geronimo and Naiche and convince them to surrender. The mission, as dangerous as any in the war, and the man at its head, would soon pass into legend.

Gatewood — tall, skinny, and possesssing a weak constitution, due in part to a painful case of rheumatism — seemed an odd choice for the physically grueling assignment.

However, he possessed a fierce determination. The unlikely hero led a small party, consisting of himself, the two scouts and an interpreter, deep into the Sierra Madre, under constant threat of ambush. As he later learned, Geronimo himself watched the men advance through field glasses, marveling at their foolish bravery.

When Gatewood found Lawton on August 3, the latter resented the lieutenant's appearance, still hoping to find and deal with Geronimo by Miles's preferred method — war.

After arguing over how best to conduct the campaign, Lawton put aside his upset and wrote to his wife, "I hope Mr. Gatewood will succeed in his mission. I will do all I can for him by making it hot for Geronimo, if I can only find where he is."

In another letter he admitted the renegade Apaches "seem

LT. CHARLES BAEHR GATEWOOD PERSUADED
GERONIMO TO SURRENDER A FINAL TIME.

to have absolutely vanished." To a white man perhaps, but scouts Martine and Kayitah found and penetrated the Apaches' camp on the Bavispe River. Geronimo and Naiche agreed to a meeting, but only with Gatewood, whom they trusted implicitly from his years as commandant of the White Mountain Reservation and head of the scouts.

With his life in the balance, the lieutenant met with a badly hungover Geronimo on August 25. The encounter, which could easily have degenerated into gunfire, succeeded because of Gatewood's calm and persistent manner. Three days later, the renegades began marching north to Skeleton Canyon to meet Miles for surrender talks.

The trek was extraordinarily tense. A complicating factor

was the need to dodge a nearby force of Mexicans, eager to kill the renegades. Another was the bitterness toward the Indian warriors from top officials of the American government.

Despite Gatewood's assurances of proper treatment for the renegades, President Grover Cleveland wanted them executed. In a wire to Army Commanding General Philip Sheridan, sent August 25, the President said:

"I hope nothing will be done with Geronimo which will prevent our treating him as a prisoner of war, if we cannot hang him, which I would much prefer."

Miles, of course, felt great pressure to finally end the matter according to the President's wishes. In a series of telegrams sent to Lawton on August 30, he ordered his officer to disarm the prisoners, then to do "whatever you think best" to guarantee that the matter end there.

His final telegram was tougher still. Many observers believe it left open the door to a massacre. "You will be justified in using any means," Miles wrote to Lawton.

A massacre very nearly occurred. That same day, Lawton departed his command's camp in Guadalupe Canyon south of the border and headed for the San Bernardino Ranch to respond to Miles's wires. In command, he left Lt. Abiel Smith, who did not feel bound, as Lawton did, by the promise to safely deliver the renegades to their meeting with Miles.

"I haven't promised them anything," Smith said to Lawton. "You . . . communicate with Miles and I'll take command."

Smith's intention was to ride into the Apaches' camp in Guadalupe Canyon, disarm the Indians, and treat them as true prisoners of war, according to Louis Kraft in his book *Gatewood & Geronimo*.

The next day, August 31, the soldiers had quite a discussion about what to do, according to Leonard Wood.

"It was arranged," Wood wrote later, "that in case of an ugly spirit breaking out during the conference or the Indians refusing to be reasonable that each man should kill the Indian next to him."

**LT. GATEWOOD, WEARING A HAT,
IS SEATED AMONG TRUSTED INDIAN SCOUTS.**

But some Indians overheard the plot and alerted Geronimo. He and the other Chiricahuas quickly mounted their horses and began riding out of Guadalupe Canyon.

With them was Gatewood, who promised Geronimo that if a shooting fight erupted that couldn't be stopped, he would flee with the renegades. After securing defensible positions for his people, Geronimo rode with Gatewood toward Smith's advancing column.

As they neared each other, Gatewood asked the commander his intention. Smith said he wished to talk to the Chiricahuas.

Gatewood informed him that no meeting would take place. Kraft wrote that Smith cited his rank and showed his temper, but still couldn't force his will. Gatewood said he knew that Smith's real purpose was to murder Geronimo, then the mild-mannered lieutenant threatened to "blow the head off the first man if he didn't stop."

The first man, Leonard Wood, backed down, then Smith did the same, and the trouble ended. The combined force of

GERONIMO AND NAICHE ON HORSEBACK.

soldiers and surrendering renegades proceeded to Skeleton Canyon.

The long-sought meeting with Miles occurred September 3. The general, terrified of a breakout that would mar his success, delayed going to Skeleton Canyon for several days, a period in which his officers and men were forced to contain the jittery Indians.

Only when Geronimo sent two Chiricahua hostages to Bowie as evidence of his serious intent to surrender did Miles proceed to the conference. He arrived in full uniform on a fresh horse, showing all the pomp and vanity of a general who did not attend West Point and was deeply conscious of it. In this and other episodes of his career, Miles earned his nickname, the "Brave Peacock," given him years later by Teddy Roosevelt.

But he completed the surrender. First Geronimo, then Naiche, agreed to come to Fort Bowie — on the condition they be reunited with their families in Florida within five days. Realizing the import of the moment, and always conscious of

NAICHE, FOLLOWING SURRENDER.

symbolism, Miles rode ahead with Geronimo and Naiche at his side, as if he alone had arranged their surrender.

The war's end drew great sighs of relief. The scourge was over, and Miles was Arizona's new hero.

Tucson hosted a parade in which the general rode in an open carriage, waving to an adoring crowd as the 4th Cavalry band played. On a specially-built stage in Levin's Park, beneath flags, bunting, and evergreen boughs, he was presented with a golden sword from Tiffany's of New York.

The *Arizona Daily Star* even urged Miles to run for president in 1888. "He does not know what failure means," the paper gushed.

Forgotten amid the back-slapping was Crook. His supporters, including many of the men who had served under him, were quick to point out all the fine work he had done over the years and to latch onto whatever thread they could to diminish Miles.

There were many. Unlike Crook, who led his men into battle, Miles never went near the Apaches until Gatewood had all but secured their surrender, and he tried to hide Lawton's obvious failure.

In *Personal Recollections*, Miles's vanity press memoirs published in 1897, the general implied that Lawton's troops had run the Indians ragged, forcing them to retreat deeper in Mexico. Geronimo wasn't going to surrender, but he talked him into it, Miles claimed.

"I had a conversation with Geronimo in which I induced him to talk quite freely," Miles wrote, "and then tried to explain to him the uselessness of contending against the military authority of the white race . . ."

The beautiful sword presented to Miles was another source of snickering among the pro-Crook crowd. It cost $1,000. But with the date of the presentation approaching, the committee of Tucson citizens in charge of raising money to buy it had only $800 on hand. Miles himself kicked in the final $200, in essence paying for his own tribute. Even more galling was what many historians view as his effort to conceal Gatewood's pivotal role in the surrender. But the issue is somewhat complicated.

In his 1886 annual report, as DeMontravel noted, Miles did write that Gatewood "rode boldly into their presence, at the risk of his life, and repeated the demand for their surrender." And in 1895, the general wrote a recommendation on Gatewood's behalf in a failed effort to secure him the Medal of Honor.

In less official venues, however, he pointedly refused to praise Gatewood. In his memoirs, for example, Miles saluted seven of his officers for their courage and efficiency, but never mentioned Gatewood.

The lieutenant's name also was absent from the roster of heroes read at the Tucson celebration. Asked about the oversight, an angry Miles said he was "sick of this adulation of Lieutenant Gatewood, who only did his duty."

FORMER "HOSTILES" WHO HAD SURRENDERED
TO GENERAL MILES WERE PHOTOGRAPHED
BY C.S. FLY IN SAN ANTONIO, TEXAS.

Also worth noting was Gatewood's absence from the Tucson event. To avoid being upstaged, the general had ordered him to remain in Los Angeles, where he served as Miles's personal aide. He was put in that job, many believe, to keep him close to the general's side and prevent him from talking to the press about what really happened.

To add a surreal note to the glory grabbing, even Lawton, who had no clue where Geronimo's hideout was, attempted to take credit for the surrender.

"You need not believe all the lies the newspapers tell you about the campaign," Lawton wrote in a letter from Fort Huachuca shortly after returning there. "I got Geronimo myself, and feel very good over the complete success of my five months' work."

Gatewood, the man who did the real work, stayed mostly close-mouthed. It wasn't in his character to boast. For his trouble, the lieutenant became a pariah for standing with Geronimo in the confrontation with Smith's 4th Cavalry, the unit Miles had hand-picked for glory. In the Apache Wars, this was a common fate for those who chose to do the right thing.

CHAPTER TWELVE

The Scent of Catastrophe

General Miles was certain of one thing: He didn't want the delegation back in Arizona, fearing their return might complicate his plan to remove the peaceful Indians from the Fort Apache reservation.

⟫•⟪

W HILE CAPT. HENRY LAWTON TRAVERSED NORTHERN MEXICO in search of Geronimo, hungry, thirsty, and utterly frustrated, Gen. Nelson Miles plotted the removal of more than 430 peaceful Chiricahua and Warm Springs Apaches living near Fort Apache.

He stated his view of them plainly in his *Personal Recollections*:

> "A more turbulent, desperate, disreputable band of human beings I had never seen before and hope never to see again. The Apaches on this reservation were called prisoners of war, yet they had never been disarmed or dismounted. When I visited their camp they were having drunken orgies every night, and it was perfect pandemonium."

As he pondered what to do with them, Miles was helped in his decision by a junior West Point officer, who, according to Miles's biographer Peter DeMontravel, offered a creative solution.

Early in June 1886, while showing the general the terrain around Fort Huachuca, the officer suggested that Miles fake a

APACHE CHIEF CHATTO BECAME A LOYAL ARMY SCOUT, BUT
SHARED THE FATE OF RENEGADE APACHES AT WAR'S END.

hostile raid, and when the peaceful Indians reported to an en-
closed area as a show of innocence, as they usually did, soldiers would disarm and arrest them. Then they could be herded
onto railroad cars and sent away.

Miles expressed horror. "Why, that would be treachery.
I could never do that."

Within a month, however, he came to accept the idea that
a permanent peace was impossible unless these Indians were
removed. How to do that without sparking another outbreak
or a shooting war became one of Miles's consuming goals.

In July, he convinced a group of Apaches to travel to
Washington and meet with white leaders to hear of the great
things the government could do for them if they agreed to move.

The 10-man delegation, led by the scouts Chatto, who
like Tzoe, had turned on his people, and Kayetenna, met the
Secretary of War and the Secretary of the Interior, and had a
brief audience with President Grover Cleveland.

Chatto was presented with a silver medal for his service.

INDIAN DELEGATES AND AGENTS MEETING IN WASHINGTON, D.C.

Like the others, he was awed by the size and grandeur of the white man's buildings, which surely was part of Miles's thinking.

But Chatto's only desire, which he expressed to Cleveland, was to return to Arizona and live with his people on the White Mountain Reservation. In a third-person translation of his plea, Chatto said:

> "He cannot make big houses like this, but can only take small sticks and make a house. But still, even if his hands ache, he wants to live that way."

Although nothing was firmly decided, the delegation left Washington believing they would get their wish.

When Miles heard of the Indians' desire to remain in Arizona, he pointed the finger of blame at John Gregory Bourke, Crook's former aide.

Bourke was in Washington at the time of the delegation's arrival, and according to historian Odie Faulk, author of the book, *The Geronimo Campaign*, "attached himself to the delegation and used his considerable influence with the Indians to convince them their interests would not be served in moving."

An annoyed Miles, tired of dealing with Crook loyalists, wrote to his wife, Mary, "I think he [Bourke] has furnished the press very unfavorable reports, frightened the Indians and in fact has done much mischief."

With or without Bourke's interference, the Indians would certainly have chosen to remain in Arizona. But what they wanted could not have mattered less.

Cleveland had already decided to arrest all the reservation Indians, including the 10 leaders, and send them to Fort Marion, Florida. Even with the delegation still in meetings in Washington, Army Commanding General Philip Sheridan telegraphed Miles asking his opinion of this plan.

Miles knew it would be popular with the people of Arizona, who wanted to be rid of the Apaches once and for all. But he worried, somewhat obviously, that the delegation, having gone to Washington on official invitation of the government, "would consider it an act of bad faith."

To his credit, he also opposed sending the Indians to Florida, where he believed the wet climate would wreak havoc on them. DeMontravel wrote that he called it "sickly Florida" and preferred the Indian Territory of Oklahoma instead.

But Miles knew with certainty one thing: He didn't want the delegation back in Arizona. He feared their return might complicate the plan he had hatched to remove the peaceful Indians from the Fort Apache reservation.

On their return trip, the 10 chiefs were ordered detained at Fort Leavenworth, Kansas, until a final decision was made about their fate.

Back in Arizona, Miles had increased the number of men at his disposal at Fort Apache should his removal plan go awry and spark an uprising.

On September 5, with Miles safely at Fort Bowie, Lt. Col. James Wade, commander at Fort Apache, summoned all the warriors to a council. Then he lied to them, saying they

CHIRICAHUA APACHES GATHER IN HOLBROOK
PRIOR TO THEIR DEPORTATION.

were going to Washington for a meeting with the White Father.

Wade told the entire group of more than 400 to pack their belongings. No weapons would be allowed, and therefore all arms had to be turned in.

The trick worked beautifully. Without their chiefs to lead a revolt, the Indians were assembled and easily disarmed, and on September 7, they started a 100-mile march to the railhead at Holbrook.

Faulk described a sad caravan that stretched for 2 miles. It contained 1,200 Indian horses, some 3,000 dogs, and raised clouds of dust that eyewitness Lt. William Stover said "rose to high heaven."

Scouts walked in the lead carrying carbines to guard against attacks by other tribes and to prevent escape. They arrived in Holbrook on September 12.

The Apaches were allowed a final feast on their last night in Arizona. Stover witnessed the scene at the Indian camp, calling it a spectacle that perhaps no man would see again:

"Several hundred fires were glowing among the low brush, and around each fire was a group of Indians, dancing and singing. . . . Drums were sounding incessantly and the frenzied monotonous chant of the Indians pervading the night air and the mournful howling of the thousands of dogs over all (they seemed to scent a catastrophe), made a curious and wonderful impression, never to be forgotten.

"All night this powwow lasted, and many of the inhabitants of the little frontier town of Holbrook spent all night watching the spectacle."

On the next morning, at a signal from Wade, the Apaches, including the Army scouts, were forced onto railroad cars, and the windows were locked to prevent escape. None of the Apaches had been on a train before, so when the cars lurched forward, they screamed in fear.

The heat in the cars became oppressive, and with no access to toilets, the stench was unbearable.

"When I think of that trip, even at this time, I get seasick," Stover wrote. "When the train stopped for the morning feed, each car had to be hosed out. Of course it was not a pleasure to have to go into one of the cars after this cleaning, but it was the only way to make it possible for any human being, other than an Indian, to enter them at all."

These peaceful Indians arrived at Fort Marion on September 20, the same day as the Washington delegation. Chatto and the other chiefs had been held at Leavenworth for weeks without explanation or word on what their fate might be. Now they knew.

In his memoirs, Miles justified his trickery with exaggerations, writing that the Indian camp at Fort Apache included "a very large hostile element" that could trigger another shooting war at any time, leading to innocent deaths.

The hostile Chiricahuas were treated just as badly.

On order of the Secretary of War, who declared them "guilty of the worst crimes known to the law," they were ordered held at Fort Pickens, Florida, apart from other Chiricahuas and their loved ones, and "guarded with the strictest vigilance." It was a final and bitter indignity. Geronimo and Naiche had agreed to the surrender primarily out of a desire to be quickly reunited with their families, but those hopes were scotched amid high-level political gamesmanship.

Whether Miles could have prevailed upon President Cleveland and General Sheridan to keep the promise he had made at Skeleton Canyon is unlikely. But as a man of high ambition, with designs on Sheridan's job and even the presidency, he made no effort. He did demonstrate his priorities, however, by ordering one of his officers to confiscate Geronimo's spurs and his rifle as souvenirs.

The best that can be said of Miles is that he protected Geronimo and Naiche from civilian authorities in Arizona, probably saving their lives. Civilians sought to take the prisoners out of the military's control at Fort Bowie, subject them to a trial that surely would have been a sham, and execute them. Contrary to orders from Washington, Miles whisked them and their followers out of the territory, causing him endless trouble with his military and political superiors.

Meanwhile, the fight between the feuding generals continued.

Within four years, the Apaches were re-united and living, under abject, even deadly conditions, in Mount Vernon, Alabama. Crook, still their advocate, traveled there in January 1890 as part of an effort to find them a more suitable reservation.

He met with Chatto, Chihuahua, Kayitah, and Geronimo, and his report of what he found was used by President Harrison to convince Congress, as a matter of justice, to move the Apaches to Fort Sill, Oklahoma.

But Democrats and friends of Miles fought the bill because it would be interpreted as a repudiation of Cleveland and Miles. The latter even testified before a house committee against the transfer to Fort Sill, saying the Apaches scouts had been disloyal and supplied the renegades with guns and ammunition.

Crook responded bitterly.

"This is all false," he said. "These stories are being circulated for a purpose."

NAICHE POSES FOR A STUDIO PORTRAIT IN 1909.

He said not only was Chatto faithful, but it was entirely due to him and his Indian scouts that Geronimo and Naiche surrendered in March 1886.

"Anything to beat me," Crook said, grumbling at Miles's opposition.

The bill failed when Crook, its leading proponent, died of heart failure in Chicago on March 21, 1890, while lifting weights. He was 61.

It took another four years, but the Chiricahuas were finally moved to Fort Sill, where they remained prisoners of war for 19 more years. By then, disease and death had thinned their ranks by one-fourth. The aftertaste of the war's dishonorable end lingered for years, and the worst of it was the government's treatment of its scouts. They became outcasts among their own people.

"There was just one good thing about being shipped to Florida and being prisoners of war twenty-seven years, and that was that the scouts were rounded up and shipped along, too," said Asa Daklugie, a nephew of Geronimo. "They underwent the same punishment as did the combatants, and probably more. They had to endure the contempt and dislike of their people all that time."

That hatred never really faded. Author Odie Faulk wrote that for seven decades the Chiricahuas were split by feuds between descendants of the two groups.

Martine and Kayitah, so instrumental in bringing about the surrender, went into old age without receiving compensation for their service. In 1926, Martine, then living on the Mescalero Apache Reservation in New Mexico, wrote to Gatewood's son, complaining that Miles had promised both scouts $3,000 if they brought Geronimo out.

"Everybody was afraid of Geronimo then," Martine wrote, "and if the government had not promised us, we would not have risked our lives."

The general never ponied up the money. But author Faulk said Gatewood's son helped get small pensions for them. Truth was, Miles was unconcerned about the fate of the scouts, in whom he had zero confidence.

"If they were true to the military, they were false to their own people," he once told the *New York Sun*, adding that he had "no use for men who would hire out at the rate of $13 per month to trail their friends and relatives for delivery to the enemy."

Throughout his life, which ended when he dropped dead at a circus at age 86, the general refused to give even the slightest nod to their contribution to winning the war — and part of the reason was that he didn't want to cede a thing to Crook.

As for Geronimo, his relationship with both generals remained rancorous. On hearing of Crook's passing, the old warrior snarled, "I think that General Crook's death was sent by the Almighty as a punishment for the many evil deeds he committed."

And in 1898, at the Trans-Mississippi and International Exposition, Geronimo ran into Miles for the first time since the surrender and angrily accused him of lying at Skeleton Canyon.

In an extraordinary exchange, a visibly shaken Geronimo spat out, "You said all would be forgiven. You lied to us, General Miles."

"I did lie to you, Geronimo," Miles responded. "But I learned to lie from you, Geronimo, who is the greatest of all liars."

"I have been away from Arizona now 12 years," the warrior said. "The acorns and piñon nuts, the quail and the wild turkey, the giant cactus and the paloverde trees — they all miss me. They wonder where I've gone. They want me to come back."

Miles laughed. "A very beautiful thought, Geronimo. Quite poetic. But the men and women who live in Arizona, they do not miss you. They do not wonder where you have gone; they know. They do not want you to come back. . . . The acorns and piñon nuts, the quail and the wild turkey, the giant cactus and the palo verde trees — they will have to get along as best they can — without you."

The meeting ended and the two never saw each other again.

Chatto and Crook met for the last time at Mount Vernon in 1890. The Chiricahua warrior-turned-scout held his fancy presidential medal to Crook's face.

"Why was I given that to wear in the guard-house?" he asked. Then, in a final gesture of broken trust, he threw it angrily to the ground.

CHAPTER THIRTEEN

The Last
Fighting Apache

His renegade celebrity was so great that author
Paul Wellman wrote a popular novel about him,
titled Broncho Apache, *which was made into*
a 1954 movie starring Burt Lancaster.

———⟫•⟪———

EVEN AS THE APACHE PRISON TRAIN RUMBLED TOWARD Florida, the war wasn't quite over. One act remained to play.

West of St. Louis, Missouri, when the railroad cars slowed to labor up a hill, a former scout named Massai, who had worked with a butcher knife for three days to loosen the window by his seat, jumped from the moving train, accompanied by his boyhood friend, Gray Lizard.

Over the next three months, crossing land they had never seen, killing game to eat, the two men traveled a thousand miles back to Apache country undetected.

They parted at the end of their remarkable journey, and Gray Lizard never was heard from again. Massai — also known as Massey or Ma-Si — went on to become a legend in his time.

He spent the next 20 years living as an outlaw in the mountains and canyons of the Southwest, raiding and killing to survive. His renegade celebrity was so great that author Paul Wellman wrote a popular novel about him, titled *Broncho Apache*, which was made into a 1954 movie starring Burt Lancaster.

The film, titled *Apache*, portrayed Massai as a romantic figure whose only desires were freedom and family in a world fast closing in. But his real life story was hardly so uplifting and forms the perfect coda to the Apache Wars.

Massai, a Warms Springs Apache, was born about 1847 in what is now southeastern Arizona or southwestern New Mexico. One of his daughters, Alberta Begay, told stories of his youth to Eve Ball, a writer and trading post operator in New Mexico. Her account, published in *True West* in 1959, described the young Apache's apprenticeship under his father, White Cloud.

He was taught to run long distances while keeping water in his mouth, to ensure proper breathing. To learn to shoot, White Cloud hung a small iron ring from the branch of a tree and instructed Massai to put a bullet through it.

If he missed, he was sent to his mother in disgrace. But he was eventually able to accomplish the task from 100 yards. Begay also tells of Massai and Gray Lizard, a Tonkawa Indian, trapping and breaking wild horses together as boys.

The military moved Massai and other Warms Springs Apaches to the San Carlos Reservation in 1877, and there, according to historian Dan Thrapp, he fathered several children.

Another source, Jason Betzinez, an Apache himself and author of the 1959 book, *I Fought With Geronimo*, wrote that Massai enlisted as a scout for the first time during the campaigns against Victorio in 1880.

Two years later, while on a scouting expedition with soldiers in New Mexico, Massai and six other Warm Springs Apaches were deemed untrustworthy and dismissed from service. The scouts were put aboard a train at Deming and shipped west to Fort Bowie.

En route, Massai learned that some of his Warm Springs band, including his family, had been forcibly herded off the San Carlos Reservation by warring Chiricahuas and were being taken into Mexico.

In an action that would foreshadow his dramatic journey of 1886, Massai jumped from the moving train, eluded capture

**EXILED TO FLORIDA, CHIRICAHUA APACHES
BOARD THE TRAIN IN HOLBROOK.**

in a country swarming with troops, and made his way safely
to the Mexican Sierra Madre.

He succeeded in finding the renegade camp, "where he
was happy to be reunited with his family," wrote Betzinez. "But
Massai was one of those restless individuals who could not remain long in one place. . . . So with his family he stole my horse,
slipped secretly away, and headed back toward San Carlos."

Massai's volatility and ability to elude anyone showed again
three years later. On May 17, 1885, when Geronimo broke
from the reservation for the last time, Massai joined him and
several other leaders in their violent run to Mexico.

But after several months, he deserted the war party and
returned to Fort Apache. "This long and rough journey gave
him further experience in traveling alone through relatively
unknown and difficult country," reports Betzinez.

Interestingly, the Apaches in the camps northeast of the
fort nearly panicked when they spotted Massai returning.

"Our Indians were thrown into fear and confusion," wrote

Betzinez, "thinking the hostiles were coming to drive us off the reservation as they had done in 1882. He calmed us by calling out that he was alone. Once more he was reunited with his family."

Thrapp reported that Massai became a scout for the second time at Fort Apache on November 7, 1885. He was then 38, stood 5-foot-8, had black eyes, black hair, and a copper complexion. His occupation was listed as farmer. When his time of service ended in May the following year, he was discharged a corporal.

Massai spent the next five months living peacefully near Fort Apache. But in early September 1886, when the military arrested all the Chiricahua and Warm Springs Apaches in preparation for transporting them to Florida, Massai tried to stir the Indians to revolt. Betzinez said he calmed down when no one joined him.

His rebellious nature, however, couldn't tolerate confinement on the prison train, especially in the face of soldier-guards who sadistically dragged their fingers across their throats, indicating the fate awaiting the captives.

Historians and writers have described Massai's escape and subsequent return to his homeland in epic terms. Surely the odyssey could have been accomplished only by a man born to the wild and wedded to its ways.

Alberta Begay told of Massai and his Tonkawa friend, Gray Lizard, finding a trail where deer came to water, killing one for its meat, then cleaning the animal's stomach and using it as a water bag. The stars guided them ever west. They knew they had reached New Mexico's Pecos River by the taste of the water.

"To appreciate this amazing feat," wrote Betzinez, "you should remember that this Indian could not read printed road signs, did not dare ask questions, had no map, had never been in this country before except while on the train. Like a coyote or a wolf, he lived off the country, remaining completely out of sight even while passing through a thickly settled part of the country in Missouri and Kansas."

After returning to his homeland in the Black Range of

southern New Mexico, Thrapp said, Massai made his way to the Mescalero Reservation and stole a woman, Zan-a-go-li-che, taking her back to the Black Range with him. She bore him four children.

One of them was Alberta Begay. She told Ball that Massai had two children by the Chiricahua woman he took up with while at San Carlos. "He told my mother that he did not steal her [the Chiricahua]," Begay said. "He never stole anybody but my mother."

Some view this and other claims by Begay as idealized at best, an attempt to sanitize her father's name. Others, including Gen. Nelson Miles, told of Massai occasionally descending upon San Carlos with "movements as sneaky and stealthy as those of a reptile," capturing another woman, and carrying her back to his mountain lair.

In *Personal Recollections*, Miles wrote that Massai would keep the woman for several months, murder her, and return to repeat the same crime.

Even though Miles was incorrect in some of his statements about Massai, including the contention that soldiers eventually killed him, at least one kidnapping episode probably occurred about 1890.

In *Al Sieber: Chief of Scouts*, Thrapp described Massai emerging from the brush near a camp of White Mountain Apaches, and accosting a young woman named Na-ta-sta-le and her mother as they chopped grass with hoes.

He caught the young woman, crushed the mother's skull with a hoe, "flung his captive on the pony and fled" to the Sierra Madre.

But Massai's criminal legacy is hard to measure. He might've been a prolific thief and killer, as his legend insists. Yet he lived in a brutal frontier, when highwaymen roamed the trails and isolated ranchers might at any time have found themselves beset by ruffians, making it almost impossible to place responsibility for certain crimes.

He also was a contemporary of the Apache Kid, an outlaw who busted free of his captors in November 1889 and proceeded to terrorize the territory. Historians and even other Apaches often confused the Kid with Massai, and the two probably marauded together, further complicating the identities.

One crime laid squarely on Massai took place in the fall of 1889. He stole two horses from the Cross S Ranch, 20 miles northeast of Globe on the west end of the San Carlos Reservation, then fled south into the Pinal Mountains. There he shot and killed a woodcutter, Sabina Quiroz.

The victim's partner, Joe Guerena, heard the shot, then watched as the renegade rushed into their camp, loaded his horse with food and supplies, and fled. In October of that year, a Gila County grand jury indicted Massai for Quiroz's murder and offered a reward for his capture.

Word of Massai spread across Arizona and the Southwest, but he was rarely seen.

In the words of painter and author Frederic Remington, who wrote of the outlaw in his book, *Frederic Remington's Own West*, he was "like the dust storm or the morning mist — a shiver in the air, and gone."

Many told stories about him, including rancher Neil Erickson. He spent five years in the 1880s chasing Geronimo with the U.S. 4th Cavalry and afterward lived at Faraway Ranch in the Chiricahua Mountains.

He said that Massai and another Indian stole some horses in Bonita Canyon in 1890, prompting Erickson and his neighbors to form a posse to chase him. They never found him, of course, only his trademark footprint, so huge it earned him the nickname Bigfoot. One rock formation in that range is today called Massai Point, in commemoration of the chase.

Such exploits earned Massai a prominent place in the imagination of white writers who found in him, with some justification, reason to cling to the still-living horror of the Apache menace.

In the summer of 1891, the *Arizona Enterprise* — under the hysterical headline, "Rivals The Ripper!" — published a lengthy screed against Massai, written by Arthur C. Russell, a correspondent for the *San Francisco Examiner*.

The story was incorrect in numerous particulars, but it captured, with appropriate sarcasm, the prevailing sentiment of hopelessness that hostilities would ever end:

"Masse is on excellent terms with another noted citizen of Arizona, of the same caliber as himself. The Kid is the celebrity referred to, and the names of the festive pair are constantly on the tongues of the isolated settlers and prospectors who are near the trail that leads from San Carlos Agency to Sonora, for they are always expecting to be the recipient of a rifle bullet from either one or the other of them.

"Some day the government will offer amnesty to these warriors, and they will come to the agency to get fattened up and take new wives. Then, perhaps after a season of peace and plenty, having in the meantime cached an almost endless supply of ammunition in the mountains, they will wander forth and kill a Mormon freighter or two and resume business at their old stand."

Russell noted that scouting parties from Fort Apache had been searching for Massai since 1886 and "probably will be for a generation or so." On that point, at least, he was correct.

Fittingly, the outlaw's death was both violent and mysterious. Betzinez, repeating a version told by Zan-a-go-li-che in 1911, said it happened while Massai was with his son chasing horses north of the former agency at White Springs. Unknown riflemen shot him from ambush. The boy, who was trailing behind his father, managed to escape.

Alberta Begay provided further details, explaining that her father was forced to kill a white man who had tried to ambush him. A few days later, a posse caught up with Massai and shot him. But his oldest son got away and returned to Zan-a-go-li-che and the other children, who were close by when the shots came.

They watched from hiding as the posse lit a huge fire at the scene of the shooting and allowed it to burn all night. When she was sure the whites had left, Zan-a-go-li-che went to the camp and found a pile of bones in the ashes, along with a blackened belt buckle known to be Massai's by a bullet dent made years before.

The story doesn't end there. In 1980, *True West* published an intriguing update, written by Ben Kemp, the son a New Mexico rancher. He claimed a posse of vigilantes, not including his father, killed Massai at the head of San Juan Canyon in New Mexico's San Mateo Mountains.

The incident occurred, according to the magazine, in early September of 1906 — not 1911. In other particulars, Kemp's account of the ambush closely resembles Begay's.

According to the story, ranchers had been haunted for 17 years by an Indian who raided and killed in New Mexico's Mogollon and Black Range areas — and was known as New Mexico's Apache Kid. Even so, when posse leader Billy Keene shot down Massai, he thought he had killed an ordinary Indian horsethief.

But two days later, an Indian woman was found scrounging for food in a barrel behind the Harvey House at San Marcial, a railroad stop about 30 miles south of Socorro. She identified herself as wife of the Apache Massai, said her husband had been killed, and she needed food for her children.

From this, and evidence retrieved at the dead Indian's camp, Kemp wrote, the posse men realized that the Indian they had killed was the same one who'd been marauding in the area for so long, and that his name was Massai.

This account comes with a grisly footnote. Now convinced the dead man was the notorious outlaw, Keene returned to the ambush site to retrieve the skull for posterity. Kemp said he visited Keene's house in Chloride, New Mexico, with his father on November 15, 1906.

As they walked through the yard, they noticed a large cast-iron pot sitting over a fire, covered with iron sheets. When the younger Kemp asked about it, Keene lifted the sheets to reveal a human head in "wildly boiling water." Keene told him it was Massai's.

In a cryptic endnote, absent attribution or explanation, Kemp said he heard that the skull had been sent to the Order of Skull & Bones, a secret society at Yale University, then on to the Smithsonian.

"If so," he wrote, "it is likely listed as the skull of Apache Kid, but it should be displayed as Ma-Si, master renegade Apache."

If the decapitation of Massai sounds like pulp magazine fantasy, consider that Eve Ball, a respected researcher, told a similar story in her book, *Indeh: An Apache Odyssey*. This work contains a fuller version of her 1959 *True West* article.

She named the men in the posse and said that she, too, was told the story of the head boiling in Billy Keene's backyard.

Massai's death, however it happened, befits one whose life was defined by mystery and an unconquerable desire for freedom. In its service, he became the ultimate betrayer — unable to stay with his own people, with the scouts, and surely not on Miles's prison train.

And when he jumped to freedom west of St. Louis, he wasn't about to live by white man's law. He remained a shadow in the wilderness for 20 years.

Whether that should be admired or condemned is worthy of a book in itself. But in a fundamental way, the Apache Wars didn't really end until Massai was dead.

PHOTOGRAPH CREDITS:

DEDICATION
Page 4   Arizona Historical Society/Tucson, #45772.

ABOUT THE AUTHOR
Page 5   Edward McCain.

TABLE OF CONTENTS
Page 7   Arizona Historical Society/Tucson, #19687.

INTRODUCTION
Page 8   Map

CHAPTER TWO
Page 21   Arizona Historical Society/Tucson, #28642.
Page 22   University of Oklahoma, #878.
Page 31   Arizona Historical Society/Tucson, #1153.

CHAPTER THREE
Page 37   Arizona State Library, Archives and Public Records (ASLAPR),
           History and Archives Division, Phoenix, #97-6270.
Page 38   Arizona Historical Society/Tucson, #28841.

CHAPTER FOUR
Page 44   Arizona Historical Society/Tucson, #41085.
Page 51   ASLAPR, History and Archives Division, Phoenix, #97-7477.

CHAPTER FIVE
Page 55   ASLAPR, History and Archives Division, Phoenix.
Page 57   Arizona Historical Society/Tucson, #45150.

CHAPTER SIX
Page 63   ASLAPR, History and Archives Division, Phoenix, #96-1391.
Page 64   ASLAPR, History and Archives Division, Phoenix, #96-1382.
Page 66   ASLAPR, History and Archives Division, Phoenix, #98-6109.
Page 69   ASLAPR, History and Archives Division, Phoenix

CHAPTER EIGHT
Page 81   Arizona Historical Society/Tucson, #19505.
Page 83   ASLAPR, History and Archives Division, Phoenix, #94-3015.
Page 86   ASLAPR, History and Archives Division, Phoenix, #97-8561.

CHAPTER NINE
Page 91   ASLAPR, History and Archives Division, Phoenix.
Page 93   Arizona Historical Society/Tucson, #25625.
Page 94   ASLAPR, History and Archives Division, Phoenix, #97-2654.

CHAPTER TEN
Page 101 Arizona Historical Society/Tucson, #78158.
Page 102 ASLAPR, History and Archives Division, Phoenix, #97-2621.

Page 104 ASLAPR, History and Archives Division, Phoenix, #97-2609.
Page 107 ASLAPR, History and Archives Division, Phoenix, #97-2659.

CHAPTER ELEVEN
Page 111 ASLAPR, History and Archives Division, Phoenix, #97-7359.
Page 112 ASLAPR, History and Archives Division, Phoenix, #97-7089.
Page 114 ASLAPR, History and Archives Division, Phoenix, #97-8548.
Page 116 Arizona Historical Society/Tucson, #19763.
Page 117 Arizona Historical Society, Tucson.
Page 118 Arizona Historical Society, Tucson, #4535.
Page 120 *Arizona Highways* Photo Archives.

CHAPTER TWELVE
Page 122 *Arizona Highways* Photo Archives.
Page 123 ASLAPR, History and Archives Division, Phoenix, #98-6059.
Page 125 ASLAPR, History and Archives Division, Phoenix, #96-2129.
Page 128 Smithsonian Institution, National Portrait Gallery, #NPG.80.245.

CHAPTER THIRTEEN
Page 133 ASLAPR, History and Archives Division, Phoenix, #96-2112.

WILD WEST COLLECTION

VOLUME 1

DAYS OF DESTINY
Fate Beckons Desperados & Lawmen

Many came West intent on molding a future,
but every chain of events has a single day,
a fleeting moment, when fate points a decisive
finger and the flow of history changes.
Here unfold 20 tales of how real-life desperados
and lawmen faced days that changed their
lives forever.

Softcover. 144 pages. Black and white
illustrations and historical photographs.
#ADAP6 $7.95

VOLUME 2

MANHUNTS & MASSACRES

Clever ambushes, horrific massacres, and
dogged pursuits — each true story catapults
the reader into days of savagery, suspense,
and conflict in Arizona Territory. If life was
hard, death came even harder.

Softcover. 144 pages. Black and white
historical photographs. **#AMMP7 $7.95**

VOLUME 3

THEY LEFT THEIR MARK
Heroes and Rogues of Arizona History

Indians, scouts, and adventurers of all sorts
gallop through 16 true stories of individualists
who left their unique stamp — good or bad —
on Arizona's early days.

Softcover. 144 pages. Black and white
historical photographs. **#ATMP7 $7.95**

WILD WEST COLLECTION

VOLUME 4
THE LAW OF THE GUN

Recounting the colorful lives of gunfighters, lawmen, and outlaws, historian Marshall Trimble explores the mystique of the Old West and how guns played into that fascination.

Softcover. 192 pages. Black and white historical photographs. **#AGNP7 $8.95**

VOLUME 5
TOMBSTONE CHRONICLES
Tough Folks, Wild Times

When Ed Schieffelin struck silver, thousands flocked to a rough Arizona mining camp, transforming Tombstone into an oasis of decadence, culture, and reckless violence. Here are 17 true stories from a town where anything could happen — and too often did.

Softcover. 144 pages. Black and white historical photographs. **#AWTP8 $7.95**

VOLUME 6
STALWART WOMEN
Frontier Stories of Indomitable Spirit

Tough enough to walk barefoot through miles of desert. Strong enough to fell a man with a jaw-crunching blow. For danger and adventure, read these 15 riveting portraits of gutsy women in the Old West.

Softcover. 144 pages. Black and white historical photographs. **#AWWP8 $7.95**

TO ORDER THESE BOOKS OR TO REQUEST A CATALOG, CONTACT:
Arizona Highways, 2039 West Lewis Avenue, Phoenix, AZ 85009-2893.
Or send a fax to 602-254-4505. Or call toll-free nationwide 1-800-543-5432.
(In the Phoenix area or outside the U.S., call 602-712-2000.)
Visit us at www.arizonahighways.com to order online.

WILD WEST COLLECTION

VOLUME 7

INTO THE UNKNOWN
Adventure on the Spanish Colonial Frontier

Centuries before Wyatt Earp and Billy the Kid, Spanish-speaking pioneers and gunslingers roamed regions including what now is the American West. Going where no non-Indian had gone before, they lived and died in a wild new world, lured — even driven — by the power of the unknown.

Softcover. 144 pages. Illustrated. **#ASCS9 $7.95**

VOLUME 8

RATTLESNAKE BLUES
Dispatches From A Snakebit Territory

Here are the stories you've never heard. Funny. Outrageous. Ridiculous. True accounts of the news, yarns, and utter lies about Arizona Territory that ran in newspapers of the day.

Softcover. 144 pages. Black and white historical photographs. **#ATHP0 $7.95**

VOLUME 9

BUCKSKINS, BEDBUGS & BACON

A vibrant collection of people settled the Southwest. They left stories of enduring a harsh land, putting up with isolation, and finding thrills in ways you would not imagine. One of them found companionship in an amiable pig named Dick.

Softcover. 144 pages. Black and white historical photographs. **#ALFP0 $7.95**

TO ORDER THESE BOOKS OR TO REQUEST A CATALOG, CONTACT:
Arizona Highways, 2039 West Lewis Avenue, Phoenix, AZ 85009-2893.
Or send a fax to 602-254-4505. Or call toll-free nationwide 1-800-543-5432.
(In the Phoenix area or outside the U.S., call 602-712-2000.)
Visit us at www.arizonahighways.com to order online.